SHAPING THE FUTURE

OF

LANGUAGE STUDIES

John Benton

Axial Publishing
South Brookfield NS

COPYRIGHT©2008 AXIAL PUBLISHING
All rights reserved. No part of this publication may be reproduced, stored in a retrieval system, or transmitted, in any form or by any means, photocopying, electronic, mechanical, recording, or otherwise, without the prior permission of the copyright holder.

Printed in Canada by Gramma Publications

Axial Publishing
PO Box 941
South Brookfield NS
B0X 1T0
info@axialpublishing.com

Second Printing – January 2010

Canadian Cataloguing in Publication Data

Benton, John   1951 –

Shaping the Future of Language Studies

ISBN 978-0-9780945-1-5

1. Philosophy   2. Linguistics   3. Language Studies
4. Method

I. Title

For Janet

"I long to accomplish a great and noble task; but it is my chief duty and joy to accomplish humble tasks as though they were great and noble."

- Helen Keller

CONTENTS

Preface

Introduction / 3

1. Searching for Core Invariant Patterns of Quest / 10

2. The Meaning of Core Invariant Patterns of Quest / 24

3. Core Invariant Patterns of Quest in the Indo-European Tradition / 31

4. The Grounding Language Universals / 41

5. Language Universals in the Indo-European Branch / 62

6. Language Universals in the Dominant Branches of the Linguistic Tree / 71

7. A Dialectical Analysis of the Investigation into Language Universals / 82

8. Features of Methodological Restructuring / 101

9. Towards Methodological Restructuring in Language Studies / 116

10. Future Possibilities for the Humanities in Education / 138

Bibliography / 152
Appendix A / 157
Appendix B / 171
Appendix C / 175

PREFACE

This study is the result of thirty years of personal and professional experience out of which arose a concern about a fundamental disorientation in the philosophy of language. This concern came into sharper focus during my tenure as a secondary school teacher of English and Philosophy. Over the past two decades, I have investigated how this disorientation has taken an enormous toll on teaching and learning language and literature in the classroom. It is with optimism, then, that this undertaking anticipates a future transformation of language instruction from junior kindergarten to advanced post-secondary levels of education, and ultimately, a lifting of education in the Humanities toward richer research and more adequate communication.

I wish to acknowledge, with deep gratitude, two dear friends and colleagues for their generous support: first, Dr. Philip McShane, Professor *Emeritus* of Philosophy, Mount St. Vincent University, Halifax, Nova Scotia, for his encouragement and guidance, and secondly, Ms. Alessandra Drage, for her critical eye and nuanced editing of the final draft.

John Benton

INTRODUCTION

This study presents a coherent challenge both to those who are presently struggling with the problem of linguistic universals and to those who are trying to find some principle of integration in the broad field of language studies. It appeals to an audience ranging from students to professionals engaged either in the fields of Linguistics and Literature or in the Philosophy of Language. The full reach of the work is summed up in the title to Chapter 9: "Towards Methodological Restructuring in Language Studies." In the field of Linguistics, the Greenberg School, reaching quite beyond previous efforts such as that of Chomsky, was looking for and grasping at a principle for methodological restructuring. However, the principle necessary for successful restructuring was not hinted at adequately either in the field of Linguistics or within the broad field of Language Studies itself. The elusive principle emerged more clearly in the field of Theology. That principle also furnished a precise dynamic underpinning[1] for restructuring language studies by bringing to light two fundamental components: first, a focal shift in grammatology (treated mainly in chapters 1-4) and secondly, a functional relating of sub-fields of language (mainly discussed in chapters 8 and 9).

The first component comes to light by focusing on the search for the genesis of generic categories of language universals. Language universals are common elements that are found in, or common elements that are related to, all languages, regardless of time and place. Generic categories of language universals are accessible when pursued "on the basis of empirical observation, rather than by speculation;"[2] that is, by focused curiosity about the existence and meaning of recurring *question structures* common to all human languages. Such elements are the objectification of two core categories: first, the experience of curiosity and wonder expressed as the *dynamics of knowing* ("What is it" → "Is it so?") and secondly, the experience of curiosity and wonder expressed as the *dynamics of doing* ("What is to be done?" → "Is it to be done?"). And so my elementary effort is to stake out a fresh and practical tackling of the problem by pointing to the rich potential

3

embedded in clues discernible in the language user's various expressions of curiosity. In so doing, I draw attention to a recurring pattern in the language user revolving around the symbol "?" with which to reveal the universal dynamic of human quest. As a result, language universals are objectified in the experience of curiosity and wonder expressed in the questions "what is it?" and "is it so?" (dynamics of knowing), and "what is to be done?" and "is it to be done?" (dynamics of doing). The symbol "?" objectifies what Bernard Lonergan claims is the "effective emergence of wonder, of the desire to understand,"[3] what Aristotle claims is a beginning,[4] and what St. Thomas Aquinas claims "[w]e can all experience in ourselves..."[5] The philosophers' agreement in principle on this fundamental point about wonder is arrived at "on the basis of empirical observation."

Now the fundamental point, as well as the problem, for you the language user, is to find a credible way either to agree or to disagree with them in principle. How? On the basis of empirical observation, by doing what they did, by attending to your own personal experience of wonder, by noticing how that experience is expressed in your spontaneous use of language and reflecting on what that experience means. Ask yourself: am I a specimen of what Aristotle, Aquinas and Lonergan are talking about?[6] And does asking yourself this question in your own words provide you with some compelling evidence that would enable you either to agree or to disagree? Moreover, serious self-attentive puzzling over the symbol "?" would open up a fresh and novel way of how to read, not only this claim, but also any claim, including the claim that you have more than animal sensibility: you have an undefined senseAbility.[7] You might then consider reading Lonergan's claim afresh:

> When an animal has nothing to do, it goes to sleep. When a man has nothing to do, he may ask questions. The first moment is an awakening to one's intelligence. It is release from the dominance of biological drive and from the routines of everyday living. It is the effective emergence of wonder, of the desire to understand.[8]

A prolonged shift to such fresh and novel empirical reading would bring you to the threshold of the universal principle of language: human senseAbility inclusive of intelligence. That meaning extends to any human language act, conventional or creative. There is the play of sense and intelligence, which pivots on the core dynamic of human quest, and when you are creative – such as in solving puzzles, conundrums, geometric problems, and so on – you give birth to an idea.

It is this mood of *self-attention* to the data of wonder that underscores the broad empirical approach taken in Chapters 1 to 6. In the manner of a detective fresh to a crime scene, I investigate the existence of empirical data of quest in the performance of the language user, as well as its meaning. This data reveals the "standard equipment" that is found in human consciousness and is, in fact, expressed in the language of all humans, regardless of time and place.

Initially, I restrict the broad empiricism in the following way: the English language is not treated in isolation, but as it is rooted in the Indo-European tradition. And so I push for data of recurrent patterns through its development beginning with *Macbeth,* by William Shakespeare. Throughout *Macbeth*, and indeed all of Shakespeare, I discover that there is empirical evidence of recurrent patterns of quest that can be cut down to an essential group. Subsequently, by ranging through the history of modern English, and, finally, through the dominant branches of the tree of human language, this essential group, two generic categories of core invariant dynamics of human questioning, are revealed in every case. Again, the first core category objectifies the experience of curiosity and wonder expressed as the dynamics of knowing. The second core category objectifies the experience of curiosity and wonder expressed as the dynamics of doing.

In light of this discovery, two strategic shifts are undertaken: Chapter 2 explores the root meaning of these core invariant dynamics of human questioning, the exploration of which is extended through Chapter 3. That clears the way to provide an enlarged thematic identification of these dynamics in Chapter 4.

As a result, Chapter 5 brings the previous chapters together to provide a precise classification of attitudes and achievements that could be considered as necessary and sufficient with which, first, to identify generic categories of language, and secondly, to ground generic linguistic performance in the Indo-European tradition. Chapter 6 extends this effort to the dominant branches of the linguistic tree by providing clear empirical evidence of these newly classified generic linguistic categories throughout.

Chapter 7 shifts our focus to the tradition of writing about language. Our earlier discoveries expose a regrettable and systematic oversight in the writing of a group of very influential thinkers[9] who have sought to achieve progress in the search for language universals. I address the problem dialectically in this chapter by noting that the writers' investigations bog down in a general self-neglect: the absence of curiosity about the existence and meaning of their own data of wonder. Attention is drawn to features of this disorientation, wrought by the dominant cultural heritage in which these writers are working.

The second component of methodological restructuring of language studies explicitly comes to light in Chapters 8 and 9, by showing how Lonergan's two-pronged principle of integration, first, Generalized Empirical Method, and secondly, Functional Specialization, furnishes the dynamic underpinning for restructuring language studies. The first principle is the basis of the focal shift in grammatology that I gradually work toward in the early chapters: "It does not treat of objects without taking into account the corresponding operations of the subject; it does not treat of the subject's operations without taking into account the corresponding objects."[10] The second principle, Lonergan's crowning achievement, is transposed to the broad field of language studies: a functional relating of subfields of language through a division of labour consisting of eight distinct but functionally related tasks that yield cumulative and progressive results.

Chapter 9 adopts a heuristic approach by providing empirical evidence in five distinct stages to illustrate how the functional relating of subfields could unfold in the broad field of language studies. The evidence provided in each stage reveals that even though a principle of integration is absent, there is a spontaneous struggle for a structure of reflection that vaguely anticipates a principle of integration, the full fruit of which is Functional Specialization.

The first stage surveys a group of journals in language studies to reveal not only various shadow zones of specialties related more to field than to function,[11] but also a collective lack of vision for a globally-organized enterprise of reflection with which to control the proliferation of literary and linguistic data. The second stage narrows the focus to one journal with which to present empirical evidence that strongly reinforces the prevalent lack of control over the meaning of literary and linguistic data. As well, it analyzes how that issue of control would invite Functional Specialization. The third stage narrows the focus even further to one article in one journal, and along with an aim that moves in parallel lines to stage three, presents empirical evidence of various "shadow" zones of Functional Specialization. The fourth stage then broadens the focus to Literary studies for supporting evidence provided by Wellek and Warren who suggest an ordering of tasks in literary studies that involve "operations of establishing and ordering texts,"[12] "the intrinsic study of the literary work,"[13] "the historical dimension, and the dimension of evaluation."[14] Finally, in a line that parallels the fourth stage, the fifth stage focuses on supporting evidence from two sources in Linguistic Studies: first, I draw attention to Greenberg's appeal for an ordering of tasks with which to overcome "the heavy inertia that retards the development of adequate archive resources in linguistics. The need is urgent for reliable, detailed, comparable cross-linguistic data, accessible to researchers by topic."[15] Secondly, I show how various shadow zones of the specialties surface in parts of Rutherford's volume of studies.

Chapter 10 concludes with a sketch of how this vision for restructuring not only would shift critical reflection in linguistics and literature to a new level, but also would transform language instruction, from junior kindergarten to advanced post-secondary levels of education. As a result, education in the humanities ultimately would be lifted toward richer research and more adequate communication.

Before proceeding, it should be noted that this work, though rounded off, is incomplete. It represents a firm halfway station to a full heuristics of basic linguistics and basic grammar. And so while the elementary aim of this book has been to identify the two fundamental components in language studies, the full reach, adequately expressed, would penetrate more fully the entire scope of grammatology both in the re-cataloguing of linguistic families and in the re-defining of the standard parts of speech.[16] Indeed, the expanded reach toward a full heuristics of basic linguistics and basic grammar would bring this project full circle. But even without that expansion, this study is in stark contrast to present-day confusion dominating the broad field of Language Studies, a disorientation that is grounded in a general self-neglect in the discussion of linguistic signs. Given that parallel efforts to address this general self-neglect are also emerging in fields such as Economics, Law and Feminist Studies[17] I am confident that this critical shift of attention will prevail in language studies in the next century.

---

[1] The precise dynamic underpinning to which I refer is primarily drawn from three works of Bernard Lonergan in philosophy and theology: *Verbum: Word and Idea in Aquinas. Collected Works of Bernard Lonergan Vol. 2 (CWL 2)*, Toronto: University of Toronto Press, 1967, 1997. [subsequently referred to as *Verbum*]; *Insight: A Study of Human Understanding*. London: Longman, Green and Co., 1957; *Collected Works of Bernard Lonergan Vol. 3 (CWL 3)*, Toronto: University of Toronto Press, 1992. [subsequently referred to as *Insight*; page numbers in square brackets will refer to the University of Toronto Press edition of this work]; and *Method in Theology*. Toronto: University of Toronto Press, 1972, 1990. [subsequently referred to as *Method*].
[2] Bernard Comrie, *Language Universals and Linguistic Typology*. Oxford: Blackwells, 1989, p. 5.
[3] Op. cit., *Insight*, p. 10. [34]
[4] Aristotle, *Metaphysics*. Book A (I).
[5] St. Thomas Aquinas, *Summa Theologia*,. 1, q. 84, a. 7 c.
[6] See John Benton, Alessandra Drage, Philip McShane, *Introducing Critical Thinking*. Cape Breton: Axial Publishing, 2005. [subsequently referred to as *ICT*]
[7] Philip McShane coins the expression, "senseAbility" in *A Brief History of Tongue*. Halifax: Axial Press, 1998. [subsequently referred to as *BHT*]
[8] Op. cit., *Insight*, p. 10.
[9] This group includes Ray Jackendoff, Noam Chomsky, Steven Pinker, Jerry Fodor, Bernard Comrie, Jacques Derrida and John A. Hawkes.
[10] Frederick E. Crowe, S.J., Ed., *A Third Collection: Papers by Bernard J. F. Lonergan, S.J.* New York: Paulist Press, 1985, p. 141. [subsequently referred to as A *Third Collection*]
[11] The term "shadow" is intended to draw attention to conventional field specialization and its limitations. Field specialization suffers from spontaneity, randomness and fragmentation causing lack of unity and efficiency in language studies. Overcoming these limitations requires a shift of focus to functional

specialization. Along with that shift of specialization, there is the need for a new emphasis on the meaning of the term functional. The new view requires us to be quite critically clear on the fact that thinking functionally about the past also includes thinking toward the future. Both the shift to, and new meaning of, the term functional will eventually be a normative fundamental attitude in language studies. See op. cit., *ICT*, pp. 209-212.

[12] R. Wellek, and A. Warren, *Theory of Literature*. New York: Harcourt, Brace and World, 1956, pp. 57-69.

[13] Ibid., the earlier chapters of Part 4.

[14] Ibid., Chapters 8 – 11.

[15] J. H. Greenberg, *Universals of Human Language*. Volumes I-IV, Stanford University Press, 1978, p. 28.

[16] The advanced component of the project, the re-cataloguing of linguistic families and the re-defining of the standard parts of speech would include the re-cataloguing of noun-types as well as research into invariants both of interrogative (pronominal and adverbial) structures across languages.

[17] In Economics, Philip McShane, *Economics for Everyone*. Halifax: Axial Press, 1998, in Law, Bruce Anderson, *Discovery in Legal Decision Making*. Netherlands: Kluwer Academic Publishers, 1996, in Feminist Studies, Alessandra Gillis-Drage, *Thinking Woman*. Cape Breton: Axial Publishing, 2006. [subsequently referred to as *TW*]

1

SEARCHING FOR CORE INVARIANT PATTERNS OF QUEST

It would seem best to begin my search for core invariant patterns of quest in a broad empirical style, in the manner of a detective fresh to a crime scene, thus grounding a higher plausibility and acceptability for the results that suggest themselves.[1] The broad empiricism is restricted in the following sense. The initial crime scene, so to speak, will be the English language: not that language in isolation, but the language as it is rooted in an Indo-European tradition. Instead of pushing for what is invariant across languages, I push initially for what is invariant through the development of a language, and so I will be considering English thus through its history. The venture in this first chapter can be summed up by the question: are there elements of language that are present from its beginning? I home in on a clue expressed by the linguistic sign for quest that punctuates the end of the previous sentence. Is there empirical evidence of linguistic invariants related to this clue that can be cut down to an essential group as I range through the history of modern English?

I forge ahead in my investigation beginning with a Shakespearean play. In a line that parallels my search, Neil Freeman observes that Shakespeare's dialogue follows a method "that colors everything the Shakespearean characters do on paper and on stage."[2] Furthermore, Freeman's strategy is commensurate with my empirical task: "The reader/actor should become a 'Shakespearean Detective.' First...s/he should spot the clues...and then...explore what they might mean."[3] Thus, my task in this chapter is to spot the clues from which to compile key empirical evidence. Chapter Two will explore what the clues mean.

I proceed, then, in the following manner. First, I tackle a scene from *The Tragedy of Macbeth* by William Shakespeare because, clearly, it is a play with many crime scenes, but also, from my point of view, it is symbolically adequate. For instance, its first two scenes begin with fundamental clues that involve patterns of quest: the witches ask "where?" and "when?" and Duncan asks, "What bloody man is that?" However, I choose to focus on Scene 3 because the characters' language is highly charged with *question types* and *statement attitudes*.

In a demonstration of power and solidarity, the witches commiserate with one another by posing questions with regard to their most recent movements while they prepare to greet Macbeth and Banquo. "Where hast thou beene, Sister? (1st. Witch)"[4]. "Sister, where thou? (3rd Witch)"[5]. The heroes, Macbeth and Banquo, enter in a jubilant mood, fresh on the heels of victory over the rebels. The eerie stillness of the "fog and filthy air" is punctured by Banquo's query: "How farre is't call'd to Soris ?"[6]

Suddenly, the mood shifts at the moment the incorporeal underworld encounters the corporeal mortal world. Curiosity, mixed with tension, escalates rapidly. Out of these mysterious and unsolicited circumstances flow a distinctly patterned series of spontaneous responses by the mortals.[7]

First, there is the tension of inquiry when Banquo experiences the underworld for the first time. Rendered terrified and confused, he is still composed enough to deal with the experience as one "that man may question."[8] A *what-attitude* takes over: "What are these, / So wither'd, and so wilde in their attyre, / That looke not like th'Inhabitants o'th'Earth, / And yet are on't ?"[9]

Building upon a formulated idea springing from his what-question about the weird sisters, Banquo shifts to an *is-attitude*: "you should be Women, / And yet your Beards forbid me to interpret / That you are so."[10] Here, Banquo not only wishes to understand what he has experienced, but also wishes to understand correctly, in other words, to arrive at the truth of his sensory experience.

Thus, Banquo experiences a pattern of events that go through three stages. First he begins by wondering about a sensory experience of particular data (the witches); he is then moved by a desire to make sense of that data: *what* 'it' is. Finally, he is moved by a desire to reflect on the truth of his making sense of that data: what 'it' *is*.

At the same time, perhaps out of impatience, or out of terror, or both, but clearly as a result of his sensory experience, Macbeth strikes out in parallel lines by uttering, "Speake if you can: what are you?"[11] Right away, we note the dominance of an is-attitude: "What *are* you?" within which lurks a what-attitude: *What* are you? Like Banquo, Macbeth too, desires to understand the sensory data presented to him, as well as to verify the truth of his sensory experience.

Each man makes enough sense of his experience (what is it?) to shift to another psychological stage in his experience of the witches. The unexpected and startling pronouncement of the prophecies revealed by the "secret, black and midnight hags" ignites a shift to a *why-attitude*. Seeking the cause of his kinsman's behaviour, Banquo asks, "Good Sir, why doe you start, and seeme to feare / Things that doe sound so faire?"[12] Seeking the cause of his alleged good fortune, Macbeth asks "why / Upon this blasted Heath you stop our way / With such Prophetique greeting?"[13] When Ross confirms the truth of the prophecies, Macbeth isolates himself from his trusted partner, and engages in a further search to grasp its causes:

Macbeth   Glamys, and Thane of Cawdor :
               The greatest is behinde .
                    . . .

Macbeth   Two Truths are told,
               As happy Prologues to the swelling Act
               Of the Imperiall Theame
               This supernaturall soliciting
               Cannot be ill ; cannot be good.
               If ill ? why hath it given me earnest of
               successe,
               Commencing in a Truth ?
               I am Thane of Cawdor .
               If good ? why doe I yeeld to that
               suggestion, Whose horrid Image doth
               unfixe my Heire,
               And make my seated Heart knock at my
               Ribbes,
               Against the use of Nature ?

> Present Feares
> Are lesse then horrible Imaginings :
> My Thought, whose Murther yet is but fantasticall,
> Shakes so my single state of Man,
> That Function is smother'd in surmise,
> And nothing is, but what is not .[14]

Aroused and shaken, Macbeth desperately seeks causal grounds behind the shocking possibility that he may become King of Scotland. In this passage he struggles to work out the underlying causes why "two truths are told." Furthermore, he is confronted by a paradox that he is unable to reconcile at that point in time: "If ill? Why hath it given me earnest of success / commencing in a truth?…If good? why do I yield to that suggestion, / Whose horrid image doth unfix my hair…/…and nothing is, but what is not."

As a result, Macbeth's wonder then shifts to action-mode in which he struggles to plan his next move. A *what-to-do attitude* takes over. Macbeth formulates two distinct possibilities for action: "If chance will have me King, / Why Chance may Crowne me, / Without my stirre." For Macbeth, the formulation of possibility lies between taking either an active or a passive role by which he could secure possession of the throne. One possible choice would be to take a passive approach to the problem and leave things to "chance." Another possible choice would be to take an active role in the problem that would require him to "stirre." For the moment, Macbeth consents to remain open to both possibilities: "Come what come may…"

Macbeth's wonder then shifts, in startling rapidity, to a series of *is-to-do attitudes* as he "tries to mentally juggle four different ideas; the attempt at self-recovery, the apology to all, ['Give me your favour: / My dull Braine was wrought with things forgotten / Kinde Gentlemen, your paines are registred, / Where every day I turne the Leafe'] the need to return to the King, ['Let us toward the King'] and the need for private words with Banquo (urging secrecy) before they leave" ['thinke upon / What hath chanced': and at more time, / The Interim having weigh'd it, let us speake / Our free Hearts each to other']."[15] The need for private words "is the first of a complex series of requests to Banquo alone, which has enormous implications, i.e. that Macbeth is urging that while they both go to Duncan they should not say anything to him until after they have talked more of the Witches and of the prophecies privately."[16]

Thus, we now have a clear idea of the type of clues we are seeking. Do these patterns of quest surface throughout the Shakespearean canon? And is the characters' language constantly charged with *question types* and *statement attitudes*? The two examples below, one from the Sonnets, the other from *The Tragedie of Hamlet, Prince of Denmarke* are offered up as compelling empirical evidence with which to extrapolate that, indeed, the entire Shakespearean canon is a catalogue of types of wonder as a desire taking over the speakers. Like *Macbeth*, these examples express invariant patterns of wonder as a desire to have an idea (What?), to seek a cause (Why?), to have the facts of some matter (Is?), to reach a plan (What is worth doing? Is it worth doing?).[17]

"Sonnet 121"	*The Tragedie of Hamlet*, II.ii.
Tis better to be…	Oh what…am I
When not to be…	Is it not…
Which is so…	What would he doe…
For why should others…?	…my cause
why are…?	Am I…?
…what I think…?	Why I should…for it cannot be…
I am that I am…	What…am I
I may be…	I know…
All men are…[18]	The Play's the thing…[19]

The next set of examples seek to show that these distinct patterns of wonder also surface in the history of English, both in the infancy of this fledgling language prior to Shakespeare, as well as in the adolescence of this expanding language after Shakespeare. In addition, the data in various ways reveal the speakers' language, in a manner that parallels Shakespeare's characters, expressing a focus on self as both subject and object of inquiry.

A first example is taken from "Cædmon's Hymn," the oldest of preserved English poems, written between 658 and 680. According to Bede's *Ecclesiastical History of the English People*, Cædmon celebrates the beginning of created things by expressing his wonder about the "origin of things:"

Now we must praise	heaven-kingdom's Guardian,
the Creator's might	and his mind-plans,
the work of the Glory-Father,	when he of wonders of every one,
eternal Lord.	the beginning established.[20]

The expressions, "mind plans" and "wonders" provide evidence of what- and is-attitudes. First, these attitudes reflect a desire to make sense of what a particular thing is, namely, "the work of the Glory-Father." Secondly, what-to-do and is-to-do attitudes are reflected by the reference to God's "mind-plans." Furthermore, the statement "the beginning established" can be likened in meaning to the statement "established the beginning of every one of wonders," the orientation of which is evidence of a basic human need and capacity to wonder about the origin and nature of things.

A second example is taken from *Beowulf*, the oldest of the great long poems written in English, composed more than twelve hundred years ago, in the first half of the eighth century. Its hero, Beowulf, faces a captive and inquisitive audience in Hygelac, the king of the Geats:

> Hygelac began fairly to question his companion in the high hall, curiosity pressed him, what the adventures of the Sea-Geats had been. "How did you fare on your journey, beloved Beowulf, when you suddenly resolved to seek distant combat over the salt water, battle in Heorot? Did you at all help the wide-known woes of Hrothgar, the famous prince? Because of you I burned with seething sorrows, care of heart – had no trust in the venture of my beloved man." [21]

Hygelac expresses a diffusion of what- why- and is-attitudes with regard to Beowulf's movements. In response to the data given by Beowulf's story, wonder as a desire takes over: as a result, "curiosity pressed him" and so Hygelac "began fairly to question his companion." Lurking within his question, "How did you fare on your journey...?" are what- and is-attitudes that reflect a desire to have an idea about the state of Beowulf's journey, as well as a desire to judge his idea of the journey to be a matter of fact. The question could then be recast as, "*What is it* that in fact occurred?" Hygelac also projects a why-attitude by confiding to Beowulf that he is the cause of why Hygelac "burned with seething sorrows." What-to-do and is-to-do attitudes lurk behind the question focused on Beowulf's having "suddenly resolved to seek distant combat...?" an action-oriented attitude that is reflected in the word "resolved." These attitudes occur likewise in the expression, "Did you at all help the wide-known woes of Hrothgar...?" For Hygelac, Beowulf has, in both cases, thoughtfully pondered possible courses of action (what-to-do?), as well as reached a decision about a specific course of action (is-to-do?), with which to aid the famous prince.

A third example is taken from the elegiac poem, "The Wanderer," preserved in the *Exeter Book*, a manuscript copied about 975, which contains the largest surviving collection of old English poetry. "The second part of the poem...expands the theme from one man to all men in a world wasted by war and time"[22] over which the speaker puzzles:

> Therefore I cannot think why my heart's thought should not grow dark when through this world I consider all the life of men...The wise must be patient, must never be too hot-hearted, nor too hasty of speech, nor too weak of wars, nor too wanting of thought, nor too fearful, nor too glad, nor too greedy for wealth, nor ever too eager of boast before he has clear knowing...Therefore the wise in heart thinks deeply on this wall-place and this dark life, remembers the great number of deadly combats long ago, and speaks these words: 'Where has the horse gone? Where the young warrior? Where is the giver of treasure? What has become of the seats for the feasts? Where are the joys of the hall?'...So spoke the wise in heart...Good is he who keeps his pledge, must never

man utter too quickly the passion of the breast, unless he knows first how to achieve remedy...[23]

There is an abundance of *question structures* and *statements* that parallel previously noted occurrences of what- why- and is- attitudes. "What has become of the seats for the feasts" is a question seeking first, the idea of, and eventually the fact about, the state "of the seats for the feasts." The speaker "thinks deeply" and reflects on the cause of "why my heart's thought should not grow dark." Again, "clear knowing," which is the fruit of the what- and is- attitude, grounds the speaker's subsequent what-to-do and is-to-do attitudes. "The wise must be patient, must never be too hot-hearted, nor too hasty of speech, nor too weak of wars, nor too wanting of thought, nor too fearful, nor too glad, nor too greedy for wealth, nor ever too eager of boast before he has clear knowing." Moreover, the speaker seeks to *generalize* in a manner that suggests a universal truth that transcends the restrictions of space and time. He infers a truth about all humans, in all places, at all times. The statements, "before he has clear knowing," and "knows first how to achieve remedy," express a clear conviction about, in the first instance, the criteria, and in the second instance, the procedure, with which to solve the problems that afflict humankind.

A fourth example is taken from the Seventeenth Century poet, John Donne. Donne's writing not only gives clues that parallel my earlier examples, but also evidence a reflexive turn in the poet's curiosity about himself as language user. In the poem, "Song," Donne wonders about how to "find / What wind / Serves to advance an honest mind." He describes his search as "a pilgrimage...born to strange sights, / Things invisible to see...All strange wonders..."[24] In "The Ecstasy," the focal point of his "pilgrimage," again, is himself, as a man of words, who is drawn toward a remote, invisible world. The following passage reveals Donne's daring attempt to stretch linguistic possibility in an effort to transcend the symbolic sensory world. His language is meshed with questions and attitudes characteristic of a bold explorer of letters, poised, facing the foothills of a dark mountainous region:

> We then, who are this new soul, know,
>   Of what we are composed, and made,
> For th'atomies of which we grow,
>   Are souls, whom no change can invade.
> But O alas, so long, so far
>   Our bodies why do we forbear?
> They are ours, though they are not we; we are
>   The intelligences, they the sphere.
> We owe them thanks because they thus,
>   Did us to us at first convey,
> Yielded their forces, sense, to us,
>   Nor are dross to us, but allay.
> On man heaven's influence works not so
>   But that it first imprints the air,
> So should into the soul may flow,
>   Though it to body first repair.
> As our blood labors to beget
>   Spirits as like souls as it can,
> Because such fingers need to knit
>   That subtle knot which makes us man
> So must pure lovers' soul descend
>   T'affections, and to faculties
> Which sense may reach and apprehend;
>   Else a great Prince in prison lies.
> To our bodies turn we then, that so
>   Weak men on love revealed may look;
> Love's mysteries in souls do grow,
>   But yet the body is his book.
> And if some lover, such as we,
>   Have heard this dialogue of one,
> Let him still mark us; he shall see
>   Small change when we are to bodies gone.[25]

In this intense reflection, Donne discovers that "[o]ur bodies… / …are ours, though they are not we; we are / The intelligences…." In so many words, Donne asserts that the illumination of mind is what "our blood labors to beget / Spirits as like souls as it can, / because such fingers need to knit / That subtle knot which makes us man…Which sense may reach and apprehend…." The tone of his language reveals a solitary and puzzled man's desperate struggle to define himself, to reach up to his own mind with such a level of subtlety as to make its apprehension accessible. Finally, I note in particular, Donne's startling phrase "dialogue of one,"[26] which anticipates James Joyce's deep-rooted focus three centuries later.[27]

From early on in his career, the twentieth century Irish author, James Joyce, was a frontiersman on a lifelong journey engaged in "a dialogue of one." His poem, entitled "Shine and Dark," is suggestive of a longing originating at the core of his being, as language-user, emergent in the question, "why?":

> The why of the world is an answerless riddle
> Puzzlesome, tiresome, hard to unriddle.[28]

Joyce makes puzzlement about himself a topic, and attempts to reinvent the English language in order to open up the topic of the puzzled self. He is, in a sense, "the literary detective of the imagination, reading the book of himself." Joyce's biographer, Richard Ellmann, describes Joyce's imaginary search to enlarge the boundaries of language as an attempt to move symbolically into uncharted "wordscape." In order to bring this about, Joyce adopted the term "epiphany" from Catholic liturgy, and ascribed to it a unique denotation:

> The epiphany was the sudden 'revelation of the whatness of a thing,' the moment in which 'the soul of the commonest object…seems to us radiant.'[29]

Along with the "whatness of things" common to all human experience, the "thing" that most puzzled Joyce was the mysterious object of "self". The search for the "whatness" of "self" was life-long. And like Donne before him, but clearly in his own right, and with astonishing powers of attention to his own experience, Joyce stretched the English language in a way that, paradoxically, pointed toward, yet led away from, the imaginary symbolic world of the senses, in all its forms, shapes and tones, toward the "yet-to-be-defined" core of his being. This resonates with particular force in the "Proteus" chapter of his great novel *Ulysses*. Stephen Dedalus takes a seaside walk, and in a dramatic moment of wonder, engages in a "dialogue of one:"

> Ineluctable modality of the visible: at least that if no more, thought through my eyes. Signatures of all things I am here to read...Limits of the diaphane...Stephen closed his eyes...You are walking through it howsomever...Am I walking into eternity along Sandymount strand?[30]

Dedalus meditates on the matter concerning "*thought* through [his] eyes," as proceeding toward an epiphany with regard to "signatures of all things [he is] here to read." Furthermore, and in the tone of one imprisoned,[31] he remarks on the "limits of the diaphane," that is, the insubstantial symbolic world represented by the data of sense. But when he "closed his eyes," he imagined "walking through it *howsomever*" and asked himself "*Am I* walking into eternity...?" Here, the detective of the imagination offers a symbolic, but fundamental clue, that the dark "objects" of the mind, deeply buried in the "eternal self," will yield "*howsomever*," the elusive definition of "self." The epiphany in this episode regards a fundamental shift – because if the mind is limited to the "objects" of the "diaphane," then the "scene of the crime," must, in fact, be the "crime of the *seen*."[32] For Joyce, the self of the mind's eye is no more than a partial constituent of the self intussuscepted by the mind's "I."

In "Oxen in the Sun," with heightened sense ability, Joyce counters the word "diaphane," with the neologistic "adiaphane," and probes his "subsolar being." Moreover, with a genius that parallels Shakespeare's prolific gift for "fire new words," Joyce molds "fire new expressions" for question structures that reinvigorate their fundamental priority in any legitimate inquiry into "self," "origin," "destiny," "procedure," and "mind:"

> The adiaphane...in the nights of prenativity and postmortemity is their most roper ubi and quomodo. And as the ends and ultimates of all things accord in some mean and measure with their inceptions and originals...so is it with our subsolar being...And...no man knows...to what process we shall thereby be ushered...whether to Topphet or to Edenville in the like way is all hidden when we would backward see

from what region of remoteness the whatness of our whoness hath fetched his whenceness.³³

Joyce points out that the "hidden" human "region of remoteness," which is the state of "our *who*ness," is both grounded and revealed by, our attitude to "w*hat*ness." Joyce plasticizes language so that this seemingly frivolous flurry of wordplay and literary allusion is shaped to mean that self is a quest-embodied being, a whirling incarnation of patterned whats and whys and ises.

This draws to a close the first stage in the search for core-attitudes. We emerge from the "crime scene" with a broad empirical catalogue of invariant question structures from the history of the English language. We note invariant patterns of wonder, bubbling up spontaneously and directly as what-attitudes and why-attitudes, and, upon reflection, terminating as is-attitudes. Moreover, these attitudes ground corresponding action-attitudes bubbling up spontaneously and directly as what-to-do attitudes and reflectively as is-to-do attitudes. Collectively, I call these invariant question structures *core-attitudes*. Furthermore, when the language user becomes aware of the spontaneous occurrence of these core-attitudes bubbling up from within, there is a revelation of the self to the self.

In Chapter 2, with the aid of Aristotle, I will begin to draw attention to what these core-attitudes[34] mean. And so I end up here with a clue drawn from a pun on Joyce's words: "to *what* process we shall thereby be ushered...."

---

[1] The presentation of data, obviously, will not be exhaustive. My case will be built on establishing reasonable grounds for extrapolation.
[2] Neil Freeman, *Shakespeare's First Texts*. Vancouver: Folio Scripts, 1994, p. 32.
[3] Ibid., p. 58.
[4] William Shakespeare, *The Tragedie of Macbeth*. New York: Applause Books, 1998, p. 5.
[5] Ibid., p. 5.
[6] Ibid., p. 6.
[7] See Op. cit., *Folio Scripts*, p. 45. The "Inner Dialogue Game," coined by Neil Freeman, provides a further valuable clue that ties in with the origin of language and the bursting forth of speech. Moreover, this exercise is a powerful technique both for digging out the attitudes we seek and discerning question types in the pattern in human questioning. Freeman describes the

process. "There are a thousand and one ways of both posing and answering questions to the...speech....If...questions are posed between each piece of punctuation, in performance the emotional/intellectual mind will continually be urged onwards, discovering as it goes. No matter how long or short the phrases, the spontaneity of thinking and discovering should be there because such questioning has the effect of forcing one thought to trigger the next." It is important to note, as we move forward, that Freeman's "inner dialogue game," the process of which is sympathetic to my claim, is based on an exhaustive study of Shakespeare's entire canon.

[8] Op. cit., *Macbeth*, p. 6.
[9] Ibid.
[10] Ibid., 6-7.
[11] Ibid., p. 7.
[12] Ibid.
[13] Ibid., p. 8.
[14] Ibid., pp. 10-11.
[15] Ibid., p. 11.
[16] Op. cit.
[17] Op. cit., *ICT*, p. 9.
[18] Stephen Booth, *Shakespeare's Sonnets*. Yale University Press, 1977, p. 104.
[19] William Shakespeare, *The Tragedie of Hamlet*. New York: Applause Books, 2000, pp. 59-61.
[20] *The Norton Anthology of Literature*. Volume 1. New York: W. W. Norton, 1974, pp. 21-2. [subsequently referred to as *Norton*]
[21] Ibid., p. 65.
[22] Ibid., p. 86.
[23] Ibid., pp. 87-8.
[24] Ibid., p. 1183.
[25] Ibid., p. 1193.
[26] Ibid., p. 1193. This has not gone unnoticed. The editor of this edition points out that "[t]he characteristic Donne poem might be described as a 'dialogue of one.'" (p. 1193) Elsewhere it is noted that "Donne's conceits in particular leap continually in a restless orbit from the personal to the cosmic and back again." (p. 1180)
[27] James Joyce, *Ulysses*. London: Penguin Books, 1986, 153. In "Scylla and Charybdis," Joyce writes: "Mallarmé, don't you know, he said, has written those wonderful prose poems Stephen MacKenna used to read to me in Paris. The one about *Hamlet*. He says: il se promène, lisant au livre de lui-même, don't you know, reading the book of himself."
[28] Richard Ellmann, *James Joyce*. Oxford University Press, 1981, p. 86.
[29] Ibid., p. 87.
[30] Ibid., p. 31.
[31] I am reminded here of a parallel observation once made by the American playwright, Tennessee Williams: "We are all condemned to solitary confinement within our own skins." This takes on further significance in

Chapter Four where we discuss Helen's Keller's ability to overcome the loss of two senses, most significantly her sight. This occurence gives weight to an advanced counter-cultural position on the status of seeing and the problem of correct understanding and the real. This issue has been coined "the myth of the eyeballs." See op. cit., *ICT*, Chapter 19, McShane, *Wealth of Self & Wealth of Nations*, Chapter 5, www.philipmcshane.ca [subsequently referred to as *Wealth*], and op. cit., *Insight*, Chapter XIV.

[32] This observation also gives weight to the counter-cultural position on the status of seeing and the problem of correct understanding and the real coined "the myth of the eyeballs."

[33] Ibid., p. 322-3.

[34] From this point forward, for the reader's convenience, we will subsequently refer to "core invariant patterns of quest" as the less-cumbersome, "core-attitudes."

2

THE MEANING OF CORE INVARIANT PATTERNS OF QUEST

At the end of Chapter 1, I noted that language users spontaneously express core-attitudes rooted in a desire to understand *what* and *why* something *is* in two distinct modes of wonder: in knowing and in doing. Furthermore, when the attention of the language user is drawn to the spontaneous occurrence of these core-attitudes bubbling up from within, there is a revelation of the self to the self. These core-attitudes are elemental to the language user's self-knowledge and it is toward the meaning of these core-attitudes that we now intensify our focus. In this chapter, Bernard Lonergan's reflections mediate our investigation from which to arrive at a clue to the meaning of what- and why-questions, a groundbreaking inquiry that originated in the classical Greek tradition with Aristotle.[1]

Aristotle makes the meaning of what- and why-questions in the language user explicit in this statement: "All men [and women] by nature desire to know."[2] But the fundamental difficulty is: how does the natural desire of language users proceed from a condition of not knowing, to a condition of knowing? For us, and for Aristotle, the clue lurks in the preceding how-question itself. That is, the clue to the meaning of what- and why-questions can be found by paying close attention to the *process* by which the language user knows what and why a thing is. And so Aristotle made his key discovery by noticing how Socrates asked questions.

Throughout Plato's dialogues, Socrates made it a practice to ask people what things are. What is virtue? What is courage? What is justice? What is science? He got his pupils to know what things are by arousing their curiosity in a strategic way. In Plato's *Meno*, Socrates questioned Meno's slave about a diagram and guided him to find out for himself what a thing is. Socrates made it clear to Meno, "that I'm not teaching anything, but everything is a question..."[3]

> **Soc.** ... I shall only ask him, and not teach him, and he shall share the enquiry with me: and do you [Meno] watch and see if you find me telling or explaining anything to him, instead of eliciting his opinion. Tell me, boy, is not this a square of four feet which I have drawn?
> ----
> **Soc.** And if this is the proper name, then you, Meno's slave, are prepared to affirm that the double space is the square of the diagonal?
> **Boy.** Certainly, Socrates.[4]

Socrates followed up his successful demonstration by employing the same method on Meno, first, in order to underscore his point about eliciting through questioning by engaging the pupil to "share the enquiry," and secondly, so that the slave's master, in coming to a solution, could discover for himself the effectiveness of this procedure. At every turn, Socrates cajoled the slave master to discover in the same way his slave boy discovered, thereby demonstrating the effectiveness of his method:

> **Soc.** .... Were not all these answers given out of his [the slave's] own head?
> ----
> **Soc.** ...if he were frequently asked the same questions, in different forms, he would know as well as any one at last?
> ----
> **Soc.** Without any one teaching him he will recover his knowledge for himself, if he is only asked questions?
> ----
> **Soc.** ...there have been always true thoughts in him...which only need to be awakened into knowledge by putting questions to him...
> ----
> **Soc.** Then, ...we are agreed that a man should enquire about that which he does not know...?[5]

In dramatic fashion, both the slave and Meno concluded their successful quest not only by ending up in agreement with Socrates on the matter of how they did it, but also strangely, by ending up in agreement with themselves. Furthermore, Socrates claimed that "if [the pupil] were frequently asked the same questions, in different forms," such a procedure would be successful "with all geometry and every other branch of knowledge."[6]

As a result, Aristotle homed in with remarkable precision on the attitudes Socrates invoked in anyone who uttered a desire to proceed from a state of unknowing to a state of knowing. According to Lonergan, Aristotle fixed the meaning of what- and why-questions. For Aristotle, it would seem, realized that the real catch was in the form of the question. It may be difficult to define this or that virtue: but what makes things hopeless is the difficulty of saying what one wishes to find out when one asks, even of the most familiar things, What is it? Accordingly, Aristotle attempted to fix the meaning of this type of question in the second book of the *Posterior Analytics*.

> The kinds of question we ask are as many as the kinds of things which we know. They are in fact four:-(1) whether the connexion of an attribute with a thing is a fact, (2) what is the reason of the connexion, (3) whether a thing exists, (4) What is the nature of the thing…These, then, are the four kinds of questions we ask, and it is in the answers to these questions that our knowledge consists.[7]

For Aristotle, any question – and so any answer and any item of knowledge - can be listed under one of four headings. Either one asks (a) whether there is an X, or (b) what is an X, or (c) whether X is Y, or (d) why X is Y. There is a significant parallel between the first and the third, and between the second and the fourth. The first and third are empirical questions: they ask about matters of fact; they can be answered by an appeal to observation or experiment. But the fourth question is not empirical; it asks for a *cause* or reason; and, at least in some cases, the second question is identical with the fourth and hence it too is not empirical, but likewise asks for a cause or reason. Aristotle's stock example, "What is an eclipse of the moon?" and "Why is the moon thus darkened?" are not two questions, but one and the same. Say the earth intervenes between the sun and the moon, blocking off the light received by the latter from the former, then at once one knows why the moon is thus darkened, and what an eclipse is. The second and fourth questions, then, ask about causes. Thus, Lonergan observes, all four questions ask about the middle term of scientific syllogisms. The first and third ask whether there is a relevant middle term (whether there is an X, whether X is Y); the second and fourth ask what the relevant middle term is (what is an X, why X is Y).

Now, for Lonergan, Aristotle's answer only raises a further question: granted we know what is meant by "What is X?" when that question can be recast into an equivalent "Why V is X?" but one may ask, quite legitimately, **whether there always is a V**. It is simple enough to substitute "Why does light refract?" for "What is refraction?" But how does one substitute questions of the second type into questions of the fourth type in such complex and simple cases as, What is a man? and What is a house? Aristotle considered that question good enough for the answer to be attempted, not in the *Posterior Analytics*, but only in the *Metaphysics*. However, prior to his attempt at an answer in the *Metaphysics*, Aristotle makes two relevant observations, in *De Anima*, and then, in the *Posterior Analytics*.

First, Lonergan observes that in the *Meno* Socrates proved a reminiscence of the ideas by summoning a slave and questioning him about a diagram However, Aristotle was impressed, more by the questions than by the alleged reminiscence, but most of all by the diagram. At least he made grasp of the intelligible a matter of insight into the sensible or the imagined, a key point of which he brings out in *De Anima*:

> [T]he soul never thinks without an image....Hence (1) no one can learn or understand anything in the absence of sense, and (2) when the mind is actively aware of anything it is necessarily aware of it along with an image.[8]

Furthermore, in the *Posterior Analytics* Aristotle remarks that, if a man were on the moon during its eclipse, he would not have to ask the first question – whether there is an eclipse – for the fact would be obvious; moreover, he would not even have to ask the second question – what is an eclipse – for that too would be obvious; he would see the earth cutting in between the sun and himself, and so at once would grasp the cause and the universal.[9] According to Lonergan, then, Aristotle claims that grasping the cause is not an ocular vision, but an insight into the sensible data. Grasping the universal is the production of the *inner word*[10] that expresses that insight.

And so in the *Metaphysics*, Aristotle illustrates this fundamental point from the instance of geometrical problems; they are difficult when the construction is merely in potency; but draw in the construction, and one solves the problem almost by inspection. Stare at a triangle indefinitely, and one will be no nearer to seeing that its three angles must equal two right angles. But through the vertex draw a line parallel to the base, and the equality of alternate angles ends the matter at once.

> It is an activity…that geometrical constructions are discovered; for we find them by dividing. If the figures had been already divided, the constructions would have been obvious; but as it is they are present only potentially…therefore, the potentially existing constructions are discovered by being brought to actuality; the reason is that the geometer's thinking is an actuality; so that the potency proceeds from an actuality; and therefore it is by making constructions that people come to know them….[11]

The result is that one has suddenly grasped the intelligible in the sensible data. The act of understanding leaps forth when the sensible data are in a suitable constellation.

With these revelations by Aristotle in mind, we, along with Lonergan, may then revert to the main problem of how Aristotle is able to transform questions of the second type (What is an X?) into questions of the fourth type (Why X is Y?) in such ultimate and simple cases as, What is a man? What is a house? Lonergan says of Aristotle that the clue lies in the fact of insight into sensible data. For an insight, an act of understanding is a matter of knowing a cause. Presumably, in ultimate and simple cases, the insight is the knowledge of a cause that stands between the sensible data and the concept whose definition is sought. Aristotle made it a key factor in his system; and it was to the *formal* cause that he appealed when, in the *Metaphysics*, he attempted to settle the meaning of such questions as, What is a man? What is a house? The meaning is, Why is **this sort of body** a man? Why are stones and bricks **arranged in a certain way**, a house? What is **it** that causes the matter, sensibly perceived, to be a thing? For Aristotle, then, that which makes this type of body to be a man, is a human soul. That which makes these stones and bricks to be a house, is an artificial form. That which makes matter, in general, to be a thing, is the formal cause.

Thus, Lonergan sums up Aristotle's position on the matter as follows. The Aristotelian formulation of understanding is the scientific syllogism in which the middle term is the real cause of the presence of the predicate in the subject. But the genesis of the terms involved in scientific syllogisms follows the same model: *sense* provides the subject, *insight* into the sensible data the middle, and *conceptualization* the predicate, which is the definition whose genesis was sought. Thus, "what a thing is" is at the very center of Aristotle's thought. It is the first and immediate middle term of scientific syllogistic demonstration; simultaneously, it is the goal and term of all positive inquiry, which begins from wonder about data and proceeds to search for a series of distinct causes – *material*, *efficient*, *final*, but principally formal; for the formal cause makes matter a thing and, combined with common matter, is the *essence* of the thing.

Thus far, with the assistance of Aristotle, I have identified two distinct core-attitudes in the language user: a *what-attitude* and a *why-attitude*. What- and why-questions express our search to understand "what a thing is." Grasping "what a thing is" is the first and immediate middle term of scientific syllogistic demonstration; simultaneously, the pronoun "it" expresses the goal and term for all positive inquiry, which begins from wonder about data and proceeds to search for causes. In Chapter 3, my task will be to establish further, both the existence of, and a direct relationship between, core-attitudes in the language user and how they are directed toward a series of distinct causes.

¹ In this chapter I draw heavily on op. cit., *Verbum*. For a full account of the meaning of what and why questions, see Chapter 1, "Definition and Understanding," pp. 12-59.
² Aristotle, *Metaphysics* I, A, 1 980a, in Richard McKeon (ed.) *Introduction to Aristotle*. New York: The Modern Library, 1947, p. 243. Further references to Aristotle's work below are taken from the McKeon edition.
³ Plato, *Meno*. 84.d.5, in R. W. Sharples (ed.) Wiltshire: Aris and Phillips Ltd., 1985.
⁴ Ibid., 84.d.10, 85.b.5
⁵ Ibid., 85.b.5, 85.c.5, 85.d.10, 86.a, 86.c.5
⁶ Ibid., 82.c.5
⁷ Aristotle, *Posterior Analytics*, II, 1, 89b, 22.
⁸ Aristotle, *De anima*, III, 7, 431a 14. Also, *De anima*, III, 8, 432a 3-10.
⁹ Op. cit., *Posterior Analytics*, II, 2, 90a 24 ff.
¹⁰ This act grounds further human acts of expression attached to the term "inner word." Their meaning will be discussed more fully in Chapter 4.
¹¹ Op. cit., *Metaphysics*, IX, 9, 1051a 22-33.

3

CORE INVARIANT PATTERNS OF QUEST IN THE INDO-EUROPEAN TRADITION

In Chapter Two, with the assistance of Aristotle, I identified two distinct core-attitudes in the language user: a what-attitude and a why-attitude. As named, these core-attitudes express our search to understand "what a thing is," often manifested in the questions "what is *it*?" and "why is *it* thus, or so?" Grasping "what a thing is" is the first and immediate middle term of scientific syllogistic demonstration; simultaneously, the pronoun "it" expresses the goal and term for all positive inquiry, which begins from wonder about data and proceeds to search for causes.

In this chapter, and in a line that parallels Chapter One, I continue to seek empirical evidence of the occurrence of these two core-attitudes, but now with the advantage of an added clue: an act of understanding is a matter of knowing a cause. Thus, I seek to establish further, both the existence of, and a direct relationship between, core-attitudes in the language user and how they are directed toward distinct causes. I do so by uncovering evidence in a Sanskrit text of ancient India, *The Bhagavad-Gita*, from *The Mahabharata*, one of the great Hindu epics in Vedic literature,[1] and relating that evidence to parallel discoveries by Aristotle and St. Thomas Aquinas.[2]

We begin by looking back at a climactic moment in *The Bhagavad-Gita* in which, Arjuna, a young disciple pausing between the armies of his Kinsmen, engages in a passionate conversation with his elderly master, Krishna, his divine charioteer. Arjuna, the wonder-struck language user, is anxiously seeking council from Krishna and expresses his inmost desire:

> My limbs sink down,
> And my mouth dries up,
> And my body trembles,
> And my hair stands on end.

> [My] bow falls from my hand,
> and my skin burns,
> And I am unable to remain as I am,
> and my mind seems to ramble.

Arjuna is referred to as "Best of the Embodied," a powerful image that underscores his presence as the incarnate wonder-struck language user. And so in a flurry of diffused wonder, Arjuna earnestly, perhaps desperately, expresses his desire to know the cause of "what" and "why" a particular thing is: "what to us is kingship?" "what joy?" "Why should we not know enough / To turn back, through discernment / From this evil…?" Indeed, the disciple Arjuna is a restless vortex of "whats," "whys," and "ises," in his desire to understand and to act, earnestly seeking "to know the truth…"

> Arjuna spoke:
>
> Material nature and spirit,
> The field and the knower of the field,
> Knowledge and the object of knowledge,
> Concerning these [things] I wish to know…³

In response, Krishna admonishes Arjuna to pay attention to himself, to attend to his deepest desires and to the unknowns to which they are directed:

> …where beholding the self, by the self,
> ……….
> He knows the location of that infinite…
> Which is grasped by the intelligence and transcends the senses,
> And, established there,
> Does not deviate from the truth…
> Sees the same (self) at all times.
> ……….
> …self in the world of the living
> …self,
> [of which…the mind]
> Draws to itself the senses…
> That exist in material nature.
> ……….
> [The mind presides] over hearing, sight and touch,

> Taste and smell...
> ...incarnated as the individual self
> [it e]njoys the objects of the senses.
> ....
> The great elements, the consciousness of "I,"
> The intelligence and...
> The senses...
> And the fields of action of the senses...
> ....
> Its form is not perceptible here in the world...[4]

From this dramatic exchange it is clear that the self that Krishna identifies, and the quest that Arjuna embodies, originate in wonder about the data of experience taken in by the five senses: that which is seen, heard, touched, smelled, tasted. Simultaneously, from this exchange, it is clear there is an inner process that searches for causes of "the objects of the senses." He asserts that the source "of knowledge and the object of knowledge" is both "the field and the knower of the field." The drive for self-knowledge and knowledge of the field head for the unknown, "beyond the senses"; "its form is not perceptible here in the world"; it is accessible only by the invisible region expressed by the words "I, / the intelligence," which point to the causes of "material nature and spirit." This core identity between the speaker and the spoken finds its elemental expression in Arjuna's question: "Krishna, what defines a man...I want to know the real essence?"[5] In other words, Arjuna's raising of the question in itself reveals the answer: The expression *What?* defines Arjuna at the core, the core of all language users.

We draw fundamental significance from Arjuna's quest for definition and real essence by noting how language[6] brings together the universality expressed in Arjuna's spontaneous patterns of quest in a way that precisely parallels Aristotle's identification of patterns of quest: first, what- and why-questions in the language user are invariant; all language users spontaneously desire to know what and why a thing is, and secondly, this activity is self-defining. With proper attention, the language user simultaneously achieves *insight* into the data of experience, as well as the data of her/his core-attitudes. Self-attention reveals that the language user desires to understand the causes of the full range of all things that exist. And so the language user asks, what is it that causes the matter, sensibly perceived, to be a thing? Each appeals to the *formal* cause in which the meaning of the expression 'it' represents the unknown cause that stands between the sensible data and the concept whose definition is sought. Thus, for Arjuna or Aristotle or any human, that which makes matter of any species of thing to be what it is, is the formal cause.

We have noted the shift between what- and why-questions. There is a shift in focus that could be represented by the distinction between "What is the rule here?" to "Why is this regular?"[7] The shift involves a difficult struggle first expressed by Aristotle, then rediscovered and refined by St. Thomas Aquinas:[8] *what* expresses the reach for essence; *why* expresses the reach for form. Both what- and why-questions name goals, unknowns.[9] These core-attitudes reflect a dynamic desire to make sense of *what* and *why* something *is*. In each case, there is a searching, a searcher, for regularity, for ruledness, for sense seeking a cause, and the causes are answers to questions. "As such questions are of various kinds, distinctions are to be drawn between different types of causes."[10]

Evidence of attention having been paid to this relationship between distinct types of causes and questions of various kinds involves a return to the drama unfolding in *The Bhagavad-Gita* with Arjuna's quest to understand the causes of all things. It is clear Krishna's responsive cajoling of Arjuna was meant to bring to light the universal human struggle to achieve a connection between these core-attitudes and five distinct types of causes. After having admonished Arjuna to pay close attention to his deepest desires and to the unknowns to which they are directed, Krishna draws his pupil's attention to five causes: "Arjuna, learn from me / the five causes / for the success of all actions...."

1. material basis
2. agent
3. different instruments
4. various kinds of behaviour
5. fate

Krishna clearly reveals a meshing of five causes and these two core-attitudes in both modes of wonder: knowledge and action, "Whatever action one initiates / through body, speech, and mind...these five causes are present...Knowledge, its object, and its subject / are the triple stimulus of action; / instrument, act and agent are the constituents of action. / Knowledge, action, agent are threefold, / differentiated by qualities of nature; / ...Listen as I tell you.../ about understanding and resolve / each in three aspects, / according to the qualities of nature / In one who knows / ...acts of right and wrong / ...and freedom / understanding is lucid... / There is no being on earth / or among the gods in heaven / free from the triad qualities / that are born of nature."[11] It is very important to note Krishna acknowledges a three-fold dynamic in the acts of knowing and doing: "Understanding...each in three aspects...Knowledge, its object and subject...[is] the triple stimulus of action...There is no being...free from the triad qualities...that are born of nature...."

Remarkably, and without the mediation of Krishna's pointings to Arjuna, Aristotle drew out these teachings as a result of personal experience in a lengthy struggle to discover this relationship between distinct types of causes and the language user's core-attitudes. In the spirit of Socrates' search for a universal definition of all things, Aristotle elevated the process to an experimental science, and as a result, brought further precision with which to distinguish four types of causes. "We think we have scientific knowledge when we know the cause, and there are four causes...."

1. the definable form [formal cause]
2. an antecedent which necessitates a consequent
3. the efficient cause
4. the final cause[12]

He refines the relationship between distinct causes and the core-attitudes of both modes of wonder, out of which the existence of a threefold structure emerges in a way that moves in parallel lines to the triple structure acknowledged by Krishna. In the case of each of the causes, we recall that for Aristotle, grasping "what a thing is" is the first and immediate middle term of scientific syllogistic demonstration; simultaneously, the pronoun "it" expresses the goal and term for all positive inquiry, which begins from wonder about data and proceeds to search for causes. Core-attitudes reflect a dynamic desire to make sense of *what* and *why* something *is*, in two distinct modes of wonder: in thinking and in doing. Aristotle observes the pronoun "it" expresses the act of understanding, "Hence each of these can be the middle term…it is from the assumption of this single middle term that the conclusion follows necessarily…the products of man's intelligence are…always to an end."[13]

Like Aristotle, Aquinas sought even further precision. "It is of serious interest to note…that one finds in each of the five ways of St. Thomas a dominance of [the] Aristotelian causes."[14] "Curiously, the order of the Ways in Thomas can be seen to be the same as the order of the [core-attitudes]."[15] Moreover, Aquinas' five types of causes (Five Ways[16] in which to prove the existence of God) affirmed a correlation between distinct types of causes and the language user's core-attitudes to be a matter of experience[17] of questions that are "directed toward knowledge of all things in their ultimate causes."[18] For Aquinas, it is a fact the "universe is incompletely intelligible and that complete intelligibility is demanded."[19] "And so in a way that paralleled Aristotle's why-search, Aquinas formulated five precise ways to structure our why-questions intending all that is to be known and to be done, by all humans."[20] His Five Ways give us an insightful ordering of distinct 'causes' that are startlingly isomorphic to the language user's core-attitudes:

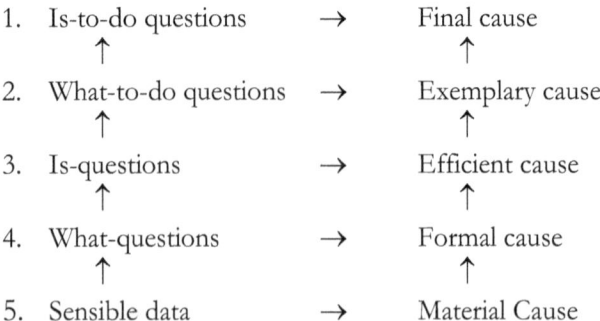

With the help of this image of Aquinas' big Whys of life, or if you'll pardon the pun, Aquinas' "word to the whys," one can glimpse the ground of such glimpsing, the ground in ourselves as language users, the relationship between distinct 'causes' and the five core-attitudes, by asking such apparently little questions as, Why is a wheel round?[21]

So, one core attitude calls for the possession of rule, form, essence, definition. Another core attitude occurs in the remark, "Yes" – or in general, yes, no, I don't know, or maybe. One moves from the suspicion about the form to the "wow!" of conviction, "Yes! I've got it!" It really is the answer! And if it really is, then 'someone did it'. Why is the wheel round? It is round because someone made it round, and we call that 'someone' an efficient cause. We have now two why-answers to the question "Why is the wheel round?" and three more distinct core-attitudes and answers can be identified with further self-attention. They are expressed in three more 'becauses': because it is made of the required raw material; because it needs to roll smoothly; because it was planned that way. Corresponding to the language user's core-attitudes we have five causes, and they have the following names: the material cause, the formal cause, the efficient cause, the exemplary cause, the final cause.[22] Keeping in mind Aquinas' insightful ordering of five causes, casting this passage as an image may help further to bring out the isomorphic structure between the five core-attitudes and the five causes:

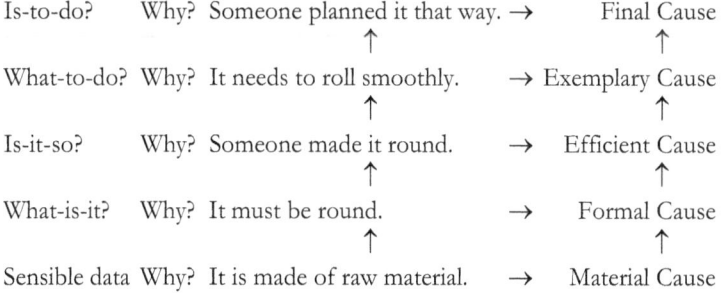

Regardless of the complexity of the data under investigation, whatever the range, from simple cases such as the roundness of the wheel to ultimate cases such as the human soul and even the matter of the divine, the language user's core-attitudes head for causes of what a thing is, and why a thing exists; in other words, in concrete instances one searches for the definition of a thing that leads, upon reflection, to a clear-headed affirmation that "it," in fact, exists.[23]

Lonergan draws on his admiration of the achievement of Aristotle and Aquinas with which to intimate his own clear-headedness about the middle term we call the pronoun "it" by pinning down, in a breathtaking sweep, the full reach of what and why questions. And so I draw this chapter to a close with the glimpse of a distant view:

> Aristotle asked what being is. But 'What?' is just a disguised 'Why?' What the question really asks for is the ground of being, and so Aristotle answered by indicating substantial form as the immanent cause of each being. His answer gave rise to the problem of the unity of the notion of being. Now if Aquinas were to ask the same question, his answer would be that God is ground of being; God's own being is identical with God's understanding, God understands himself, and so he understands his own power, and so he understands all that by that power could be produced. God, then, is the act of understanding that grasps everything about everything. The content of the divine act of intellect is the idea of being and so, precisely because our intellects are potential, they can define being only at a second remove as whatever is to be known by intelligent grasp and reasonable affirmation.... To set aside this dynamism is to nullify not only what lies beyond conceptual contents but also the intention of being itself. In a famous little treatise, Aquinas had remarked, '*Essentia dicitur secundum quod per eam et in ea ens habet esse.*' It is in and through essences that being has existence. Hence, being apart from essence is being apart from the possibility of existence; it is being that cannot exist; but what cannot exist is nothing, and so the notion of being apart from essence is the notion of nothing.[24]

Thus, in Chapter 4, we will be able to consolidate the clues we have collected so far with which to give an enlarged thematic identification of the dynamism identified by Lonergan in the passage above. For the empirical evidence supporting the existence of that dynamism allows us to make the following observations about it with confidence: it is the zone of SenseAbility that grounds the structure and meaning of our knowing and doing that we have named our core-attitudes; finally, because they exist in all language users, they ground the linguistic universals we have been seeking; for they define the process Arjuna incarnated, Krishna acknowledged, Aristotle discovered, and Aquinas refined.

---

[1] *The Bhagavad-Gita*, p. 9. Winthrop Sargeant (trans.), State University of New York Press, 1984.
[2] Again, I will be drawing from op. cit., *Verbum*, Chapter 1, "*Verbum*: Definition and Understanding," pp. 12-59.
[3] Op. cit., *The Bhagavad-Gita*, pp. 37, 662 (XVIII.1), 37, 67-8 (I.31-32), 70 (I.32), 74 (I. 36), 75 (I. 37), 77 (I. 39), 662 (XVIII.1), 528 (XIII first stanza unnumbered)
[4] *Ibid.* 592 (XV.3) 292 (VI.21) 300 (VI.29) 596 (XV.7) 598 (XV.9) 533 (XIII.5)
[5] *The Bhagavad-Gita*, p. 37 (II.54), 143 (XIIX.1) Stoler Millar, Barbara. (trans.) New York: Bantam Books, 1986. On the meaning of "essence," see *Verbum*, p. 15 ff.
[6] Relevant here is the twist on these words that echoes the neologism "How-Language." See the chapter "How-Language: Works?" in op. cit., *BHT*, pp. 49-79.
[7] See Ibid., p. 54. "The work involved is one of the most refined struggles of self-discovery, a struggle with a long history of avoiding the struggle as it was originally expressed by Aristotle." The culture of avoiding the struggle in language studies is our focus in Chapter 7.
[8] There is value in repeating McShane's footnote in ibid., p. 54. "See B. Lonergan, *Verbum*. One might begin with the discussion of Chapter 1, especially the section titled 'Quod Quid Est'." One will find a refined analysis of the distinction between form and essence that cannot be enlarged on here. See op. cit., *Verbum*, pp. 28-29 ff. "Very accurately Aquinas hit upon the root of the confusion with respect to form and essence. That transposition is from formal cause to essence or quiddity [essence and quiddity mean the same thing]."
[9] See op. cit., *BHT*, p. 54.
[10] See op. cit., *Insight*, p. 651 [674].
[11] Op. cit., Stoller Miller, *Bhagavad-Gita* (XIIX.72), p. 153 ff.
[12] Op. cit., *Posterior Analytics*, 94a, II.iv.20-25, p. 170. A detailed presentation of Aristotle's four causes takes us too far afield, for we are interested, not in the content *per se*, but in the underlying dynamics suggested by the structure of the four causes that the language user can identify spontaneously occurring in her/himself. In addition to the key passages of Aristotle cited in this text, commentary and key passages relating to Aristotle's four causes are cited in op. cit., *Verbum*.
[13] Ibid., *Posterior Analytics*.

[14] Philip McShane, Cantower XIX, www.philipmcshane.ca, October 2003, p. 9.
[15] Op. cit., *ICT*, p. 96.
[16] Likewise, a detailed presentation of the *Five Ways* takes us too far afield, for we are interested, not in the content *per se*, but in the underlying dynamics suggested by the structure of the *Five Ways* that the language user can identify spontaneously occurring in her/himself. See St. Thomas Aquinas, *Summa Theologiae* (The First Part, question 2, article 3). The reader's slow intussusception of Philip McShane's presentation in a 1958 essay of St. Thomas' *Five Ways* in op. cit., Cantower XIX is highly recommended.
[17] Op. cit., *Verbum*, p. 38.
[18] Op. cit., *Insight*, p. 407 [432]. The full extent of the nature of causality far exceeds the scope of this book, let alone this chapter, so I refer the reader to op. cit., *Insight*, particularly Chapter 19, "General Transcendent Knowledge." However, I would note that expansion on the topic of causality as it relates to language will give birth to heuristic structures in the future, the expression of which is what Lonergan has identified as "linguistic feedback." Gradually, language users in all lines of human inquiry will be systematically tapping its potential. When that happens, human language will have assumed its proper function of facilitating a massive transformation of human culture. And although the emergence of a new linguistic feedback is now the stuff of fantasy, an unrealized ideal, that fantasy can and will come into being. This study represents a modest beginning. When our use of language insightfully draws on, and draws out, the rhythms of the language user's core invariant patterns of quest, then our human culture will be placed on a luminous new foundation. For a brief sketch of one aspect of that new foundation, see op. cit., *ICT*, pp. 93-94, Chapter 24, "An International Ethic." That chapter anticipates the future complement to this book that is also discussed in the final paragraph of our Introduction.
[19] Op. cit., *Insight*, p. 678 [700].
[20] Op. cit., *ICT*, pp. 90-95
[21] Ibid., pp. 55-56.
[22] Ibid.
[23] A brief account of "reflection" and "affirmation" associated with the verb "is" will be given in Chapter 4.
[24] Op. cit., *Insight*, p. 371 [395].

4

THE GROUNDING LANGUAGE UNIVERSALS⎯⎯⎯

This chapter marks a strategic shift to the problem of the genesis of language in the human. What this chapter adds to the previous three is an enlarged thematic identification of the core-attitudes as the basis for the grounding language universals.[1] Recall our position that the principle of language is the play of human sensibility and intelligence we named senseAbility. Our meaning extends to any language act, conventional or creative, the meaning of which sets the stage for our strategy, as well as for an appeal:

> But what is that play when we speak adequately about language universals, and what is that play in the first sudden event of language learning? These are the two questions on which the remainder of the chapter focuses. There is the first bang, which we will consider shortly. There is the larger bang that will be the concluding topic of the chapter: a cultural bang that grounds adequate speech about language, its acquisition, its universals.
>
> We may lead into our considerations of the first bang, our first event that shifted us from babbling to talk, by reflecting a little more on our problem-solving experiences. There is a sense in which each puzzle solved, in geometry, in life, is a shift from babbling to talk. You can surely recall a teacher who babbled because a puzzle wasn't really solved? Or you may even have discomforting memories of "babbling on" precisely because you didn't have a clue? So, here, I need a certain tolerant openness about our next venture...."[2]

The focus of the venture, then, may be summed up by asking: What happened to Helen Keller? How do we as infants move from babbling to talk? Our full venture here will slowly pace along with Helen and our infant/childhood selves, and along with that pacing, we will weave in some supporting refinements from Aristotle, Aquinas and Lonergan with which to reinforce key elements we brought to light in earlier chapters. The result of our pacing along with Helen anticipates the breakthrough to follow; namely, the grounding language universals are in fact, the five core-attitudes expressed by all language users. Thus, the five core-attitudes[3] shown below, spontaneously recurred in Helen and in our infant/childhood selves before, during and after the first sudden event of language learning, and recurred in all subsequent events of language acquisition in a series of shifts from babbling to talk:[4]

The Dawning of Five Core Attitudes in Helen Keller and Our Infant/Childhood Selves

What happened to Helen Keller? The basic relevant facts are easily recalled. Annie Sullivan arrived on March 5th, 1887 to face the challenge of someway bringing Helen to language. One of Annie's early gestures was the signing of w-a-t-e-r into Helen's hand. It was April 7th before it dawned on Helen what this gesturing was about. Between March 5th and April 7th a cumulative series of core-attitudes arose in Helen, in a series of shifts from babbling to talk, out of which a first word was correctly understood and then acted upon. The moment of discovery was a hand washing; immediately following the discovery, Helen hastened to the discovery of twenty or so words. This making sense, by way of understanding and using words, allowed her to make the choice to greatly expand her ability to communicate with her teacher and her family. Later, when she learned to read and to write, she had access to the written records of human meanings, with which to bring about an astonishing enrichment to her life.

1. Sensible Experience

The steady stream of sense experience is the first core attitude that occurred in Helen. Recalling Aristotle's observation, Lonergan notes, "a person without sense perception would never learn anything or understand anything."[5] Seven-year-old Helen was blind, deaf and mute, and as a result, prior to April 5th, 1887, she had not demonstrated the usual capacity for naming things. Helen recalls,

> Have you ever been at sea in a dense fog, when it seemed as if a tangible white darkness shut you in, and the great ship, tense and anxious, groped her way toward the shore with plummet and sounding-line, and you waited with beating heart for something to happen? I was like that ship before my education began, only I was without compass or sounding-line, and had no way of knowing how near the harbour was. 'Light! give me light!' was the wordless cry of my soul...[6]

Helen's days were lived out in what may be described as routine patterns for which the maintenance of physical well being, play, and fun for its own sake was her primary goal. While she did demonstrate emotions, feelings, insecurities and longings, she recalls that her way of coping and communicating involved a familiarity with patterns of touch: "I would imitate what I wanted."[7] Her teacher, Annie, observed, "When she wants to know the name of anything, she points to it and pats my hand,"[8] [and] "Although Helen quickly imitated the hand signs, she made no connection between them and the objects they symbolized..."[9]

And so within the inarticulate blind girl - skin-deep and skin-shallow - there was a lightless viewpoint: she had, or was, a point of view. Or should we rather say a zone of view, a zone of reviewing, reaching, dawning? Certainly it is fair to say the child was not 'mindless'. There was within Helen's senseAbility a reaching and a frustration distinctly beyond the subtle sensitivity of cat, great or small. Take, for instance, Helen's view of water. There are the years of liquid-experiences, of drinking and washing, splashing and bathing, tasting and smelling, pouring and flowing, hot and cold, soapy and soupy. Helen, one can surmise, had "it" all together, where "it" is the vague "liquidentity" of her viewzone - and so with other fragments of experience.

Let us home in on Helen's sense experience with a diagram. We have a triple sequence:[10]

y y   y y y   yyyy...

x x x x x x x x x x x x x x x...

zzzzzzzzzzzzzzzzzzzzzzzzzzzzzz ...

What do the first two sequences represent? The sequence z represents Helen's normal flow of sensitive consciousness. The sequence x represents the added element in that consciousness due to the hand-touchings of Annie Sullivan. The first x, corresponding to Annie's hand-touchings w-a-t-e-r, is the aggregate of neurophysiological events consciously received by Helen. The sequence x is an irregular sequence, not in fact paralleling z, but far sparser. Annie's hand touching had riveted Helen's attention and evoked wonder; her "whole attention [was] fixed upon the motions of her fingers."[11]

The image below represents the first stage of Helen's experience – a dominance of the senses and wonder. This is the first of five basic attitudes that can be associated with five meanings of the word why. It marks the beginning to making sense of our experience, the occurrence of which we associate with the material cause. Note the arrow (above) shows that Helen's conscious struggle toward learning her first word is only beginning; as wonder is aroused, further "mindful" activity lies ahead.

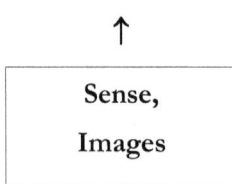

2. What-Questions

The spontaneous rise of wonder triggers the second core attitude in both Helen and ourselves. That attitude is expressed in what and why questions.[12] In his great work, *Summa Theologiae*, Aquinas draws out the fundamental significance of Annie's hand touching by answering the question, "Whether we need a diagram or phantasm to understand?" Aquinas observed, "anyone can experience this of himself, that when he tries to understand something, he forms certain phantasms to serve him by way of examples, in which as it were he examines what he is desirous of understanding. For this reason, it is that when we wish to help someone to understand something, we lay examples before him, from which he forms phantasms for the purpose of understanding."[13] The patterns formed by Annie's steadfast hand touching served as examples from which Helen could form phantasms for herself.

Helen's struggle for phantasm at this stage of her journey could be summed up for us in the words, "What the heck is going on?" The "heck" hints at moods and moodswings, for we must struggle here with the reality of Helen having no words, only minded moods. Why do we start the y sequence later than the sequence x?

y y   y y y   yyyy…

x x x x x x x x x x x x x x x…

zzzzzzzzzzzzzzzzzzzzzzzzzzzzzz …

We allow for the possibility that the initial addition of the x sequence to Helen's life was accepted as merely the addition of a game, a finger game. After a couple of weeks, especially with the shift of locale and of style of life, the fun would surely fade!

No doubt the fun was replaced by Helen's struggle to make sense of such things as 'mug' and 'milk;' "they had given her trouble. She confused the nouns with the verb 'drink.'[14] This struggle could be observed in her body language, simultaneously connoting confusion and frustration. Helen recalls, "Earlier in the day we had had a tussle over the words 'm-u-g' and 'w-a-t-e-r.' Miss Sullivan had tried to impress it upon me that 'm-u-g' is mug and that 'w-a-t-e-r' is water, but I persisted in confounding the two."[15] But it is the state of wonder that begins to dominate, stimulated by memories of prolonged contact with varieties of liquids throughout her childhood, and further awakened by the added element impressed on her consciousness due to the frequent hand touching of Annie. This aggregate of neurophysiological events was intussuscepted into Helen's normal flow of sensitive consciousness.[16]

Helen's moods and moodswings were aroused by the drive to make sense of her experience. Her whole attitude could be summed up in the following words: "What is going on?" At some stage in the five weeks leading up to the breakthrough on that April day, Helen's stretching quest shifted to a why-question. Her attitude took on the dynamic of a subcutaneous quest; a fuller meaning was lurking subcutaneously. This attitude brings us to our y sequence, diagrammed as coming in later:

$$y\,y \qquad y\,y\,y \qquad yyyy\ldots$$

$$x\,x\,x\,x\,x\,x\,x\,x\,x\,x\,x\,x\,x\,x\,x\ldots$$

$$zzzzzzzzzzzzzzzzzzzzzzzzzzzzzzz\,\ldots$$

That sequence represents Helen's stretching "why?" which began at some stage in the five weeks: perhaps the sequence has only one member, a blossoming "y" on that wondrous April day. She struggled for insight into phantasm with an active, reaching, senseAbility, self-directed to the 'what' of why-answers, toward an 'it' that was a vague liquid entity. Helen whatted over sequences, in a manner that can be expressed by "why?": why the hand-shaping? So, the second attitude calls for the possession of rule, form, essence, definition, in search of a cause.

So, y is hovering over, in, the pair x and z. And then comes the dawning, lifting Helen into a new human horizon: X POINTS TO Z, one aggregate of sensitive events points to another. Well, not quite. The pointing is more complex: x points to z within Helen's zoneview. The vague liquidentity as thus meant-held by Helen has A NAME.

The name means, points. To what does the name point? It points to Helen's zoneview. It points to the grasp of something splashing, soaping, smelling over years. What does "water" point to? Most obviously, it points to water of some kind. What does "water" mean? It means either "just any water" or perhaps "what we commonly mean by water." Because Helen's grasp of what we commonly mean by water is, in Lonergan's words, "similar in all respects, then they do not differ in idea, in essence, in nature, or in any accidental characteristic; there is mere material multiplication. [Thus, Helen's discovery of the name and meaning for 'water'] can be accounted for by the reflection of intellect back to phantasm where the many instances of the one idea are represented."[17] Phantasm, then, is involved in the genesis[18] of names and the meaning they represent.[19]

We have classified a particular attitude that is summed up in the word "whatting." The attitude in Helen that we named whatting led her to the basic insight of language. And so the sensation of Annie's spelling of the word w-a-t-e-r worked simultaneously with cold water rushing over her hand and all the memories of the varieties of liquid that Helen routinely experienced since birth converged in a drive of at least one, if not more, why questions toward the named identity of the liquid entity. The motion of Annie's fingers and the sensation of liquidity had combined to provide an image or diagram, that served, in the words of Aquinas, as examples in which she may – by inspection, as it were – reach that which she is striving to understand. And so for Lonergan, "one cannot understand without understanding something; and the something understood, the something whose intelligibility is actuated, is the phantasm."[20] For Helen and ourselves, then, the act of formulating is a personal inner achievement resulting from direct insight into phantasm,[21] the goal towards which what and why questions tend.[22] In other words, what- and why-questions seek to formulate an idea of what a thing is. Aquinas named the achievement of that goal an inner word.[23] The inner word is a formulation or definition or concept.

The image below represents *the second stage* of Helen's state of wonder dominated by her what-attitude. The what-question is the second of five basic attitudes that can be associated with five meanings of the word why. It is the second drive toward making sense of our experience, the occurrence of which we associate with the formal cause. The arrow below the box denotes the relationship between the first and second stages. The arrow above the box indicates that the process of Helen's conscious struggle to learn her first word is still not complete – a further, third, mindful stage exists in her drive to master her first word.

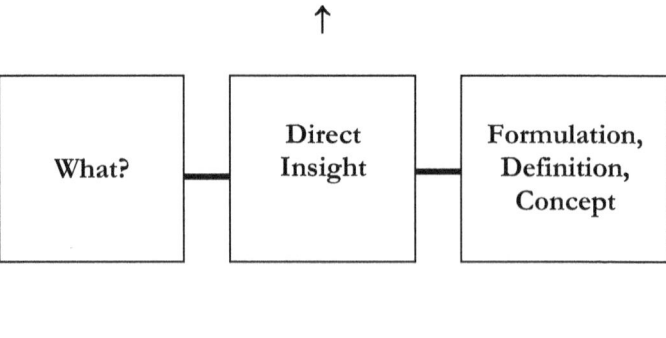

3. Is-Questions

And so now we push on to grapple with a further third attitude, present in Helen's puzzling, but regularly unnoticed. There is a long history of that lack of attention, of which, fortunately, Aquinas avoided. He distinguished the existence of two acts of understanding: the direct act and the reflective act. The first act he referred to as the expression of a first inner word occurs at the level of "whatting." The second act, the attitude we speak of here, he referred to as the expression of a *second inner word* occurs at the level of "ising."[24] In other words, what Aquinas discovered empirically was a distinction between the meaning of what- and why-questions, and the meaning of is-questions. For Aquinas, "both acts of understanding have their instrumental or material causes," but, as we have seen, "the direct act has this cause in a schematic image or phantasm, while the reflective act reviews not only imagination but also sense experience, and direct acts of understanding, and definitions, to find in all taken together the sufficient ground or evidence for a judgment of fact. Hence, while the direct act of understanding generates in definition the expression of the intelligibility of the phantasm, the reflective act generates in judgment the expression of consciously possessed truth through which reality is both known and known to be known."[25] In Aquinas's terms: the first inner word answers the question, *Quid sit?* The second inner word answers the question, *An sit?*[26]

Helen, then, is on the trail of expressing a second inner word. She puzzles, What *is* this sequence of Annie's hand-shapings? Signing? Notice that "signing" here is qualified by a question mark, marking this different attitude from the previous whatting question mark. This second case, poise, question markedness, is a case of is?-poise. There was little hesitation in Helen and she moved spontaneously into a new poise, an is-attitude. Our problem here, of course, is hesitation, where we give that word a very positive meaning of sticking, being stuck. By we, we mean Helen and ourselves shifting without hesitation to the is-ing attitude. And so we scrutinize this most difficult core attitude further.

We have explored how Helen had achieved a direct insight, had formulated a first inner word and had arrived at a possible answer to the name and meaning of w-a-t-e-r. Recall that Aquinas distinguished her what-attitude to be possession of a cause in a schematic image or phantasm yielding a solution or a hypothesis. But what happened next? She was not certain about her "hypothesis." Spontaneously, her core humanity was not content to leave things at that. She wanted to know if her hypothesis or "idea" was correct. In fact, she spontaneously wondered further, nursed a different question, seeking a higher formulation for truth: Is this it? Have I got it? Helen's is-questions, then, expressed or revealed a desire in her for correct affirmation. And so she spontaneously reviewed not only her imagination but also her sense experience, her direct acts of understanding, and definitions, to find in all taken together the sufficient ground or evidence for a judgment of fact.

The judgment of fact is the third of five basic attitudes that can be associated with five meanings of the word why. Earlier, Helen whatted over sequences, in a manner that can be expressed by "why?": why the hand shaping? She was a searcher, searching for regularity, for ruledness, for sense. Now we identify a further attitude noted with Helen's "signing?" question mark. The answer to the mark in Helen is the remark, "Yes!" In that activity of identifying, the idea is represented by another cause, an activity that is variously called noun-ing, naming, it-ing, thing-ing, is-ing. At the moment of Helen's Yes!-achievement, Annie observed amazedly, "A new light came into her face." And, of course,

Helen recalled that moment with a new joy, exclaiming "I knew that water meant the wonderful cool something that was flowing over my hand"[27] "the mystery of language was revealed to me."[28]

The image below represents *the third stage* in Helen's stages of wonder described above. We have all experienced for ourselves that when we respond to is-questions, we typically come up with "yes" or "no" answers. Where we consistently arrive at some sort of solution or description or explanation in response to our what-questions, we would notice that our is-questions invariably end with a "Yes," or a "No," or an "I don't know."[29] Or we might notice our own spontaneous gestures in answer to is-questions – a nod, a shake of the head, a shrug of the shoulders. The arrow below the box denotes the relationship between the second and third stages. The is-wonder is the third of five basic attitudes that can be associated with five meanings of the word why. It is the fifth drive toward making sense of our experience, the occurrence of which we associate with the efficient cause. For Helen and ourselves, sense experience, the light of intellect, insight into phantasm, act of defining thought, reflective reasoning and understanding, acts of judgment are all core psychological facts.[30]

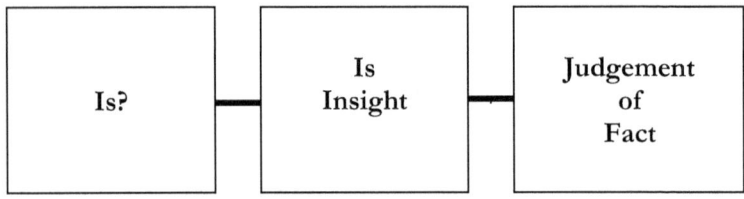

At this stage of our venture, we have an enlarged thematic identification of the first three core attitudes as the basis for the grounding language universals on the basis of asking: What happened to Helen Keller? How do we as infants move from babbling to talk? We have drawn attention to the fact that these three core attitudes spontaneously arose in Helen, and arise in our infant selves, in a series of shifts from babbling to talk. And so Helen observes: "…whatever the process, the result is wonderful."[31] Indeed, so is the process itself.

4. What-is-to-be-done?[32]

Our enlarged thematic identification of core attitudes as the basis for the grounding language universals now takes us beyond the initial acquisition of language in Helen, and our infant selves, to its consequences, the event of which yields two further core psychological facts. It begins with a *fourth stage of wonder* that takes place in seven-year-old Helen and emerges at some point in our childhood selves. For Helen, then, the initial acquisition of language leads to a further shift from babbling to talk on that momentous day:[33] the dynamic process called the *action mode of wonder*. Helen's life is carried forward; and the shift to the action mode of wonder is a deep change, a lift in life mediated by a preceding pivotal word-grounding insight that exploded into a judgment of fact. We identify in Helen's journey, and our own, the categories involved in this process and the core attitudes that spontaneously occur when the language user comes to make a *choice* or *decision*.

The thematic basis for the action mode of wonder has its origins in the meticulously detailed empirical observations of Aquinas, and he expresses its essential elements in condensed form below:

> Choice adds to consent the notion of a special relationship to that which is preferred to something else, and accordingly a choice still remains open after consent. For it may well happen that deliberation discloses several means, and since each of these meets with approval, consent is given to each; later preference is given to one and it is chosen. But if one alone meets with approval, then consent and choice coincide in point of fact, though they remain distinct meanings, for we think of consent as approval, and of choice as a preference.[34]

Cast into Aquinas' terms, then, Helen's core attitudes have evolved to a point in which her *consent* to this matter of language learning has suddenly become the center of her life. It happens that Helen's spontaneous deliberation at this point in her journey of discovery discloses that there is a *means* to an *end* that is a consequence of her having achieved a judgment of fact. And Helen's "mind was full of the prospective joys"³⁵ that that consequence brings. Thus, Helen deliberates on *possibilities* for an end of which the initial acquisition of language provides the means. Her goal is to choose an end that is *responsible, good, worthwhile,* of *value*. Helen's wonder is *practical* and, although she could not articulate that wonder in language, later she recalled: "unless I turn my glad thoughts into practical living and till my own field, I cannot reap a kernel of the good."³⁶

As a result, the first group in a series of attitude shifts in the *action mode of wonder* reflects Helen's on-the-spot desire to consent (to her new reality). And Helen's mood shift to this mode of wonder is caused by the judgment of fact that she "knew then that "w-a-t-e-r" meant the wonderful cool something that was flowing over [her] hand. That living word awakened [her] soul, gave it life, hope, joy, set it free!"³⁷ Helen reflects on other *known facts*: she quickly affirms that her blindness and deafness are "barriers that could in time be swept away,"³⁸ because she discovers that, in fact, she can draw on the sense perceptions of smell, taste and touch and achieve the same result as if she could see and hear. *The first attitude shift* in the action mode of wonder, then, simultaneously carries Helen further forward to a state of alert *sensibility* that ushers forth *images* of possibilities: "As we returned to the house every object which I touched seemed to quiver with life. That was because I saw everything with the strange, new sight that had come to me."³⁹

The prompting of fresh senses and images, along with her possession of known facts, propels Helen to *the second shift in attitude*. Suddenly her "field of inquiry [had] broadened"⁴⁰ in an urgent search to discover by what means she would go forward in her life. Helen's practical search spontaneously percolates in *what-to-do questions* creatively directed toward her new future, to what might be; yet at this stage of her deliberations, she has no *concrete idea* of what course of action she might take.

Her practical what-to-do search rapidly leads to *the third attitude shift*, an achievement of *direct insights* into her known facts, senses, and images, to bring to light possible ideas for a plan of action. She pulls together numerous direct insights that occur because of "a habit learned suddenly at that first moment of release and rush into the light. With the first word I used intelligently, I learned to live, to think, to hope."[41] That luminous new habit is an achievement in Helen that finds its expression in at least one clearly *formulated possibility*, a plan that marks *the fourth attitude shift*: "I had now the key to all language, and I was eager to learn to use it."[42] In her deliberations to this point, Helen acknowledges, "At the beginning I was only a little mass of possibilities."[43] Out of that "mass of possibilities" Helen reaches consent, the achievement of which is the prospect of an exciting new direction in her life: "I left the well-house eager to learn. Everything had a name, and each name gave birth to a new thought."[44]

Helen's what-to-do search yields a possibility for action, but she has yet to act on it. A further series of attitude shifts in Helen lie ahead. This draws out an important distinction made by Aquinas: the process of arriving at consent "involves a special relationship to that which is preferred to something else, and accordingly a choice still remains open after consent. For it may well happen that deliberation discloses several means, and since each of these meets with approval, consent is given to each."[45] In proclaiming herself to be "a little mass of possibilities," Helen's deliberation, indeed, could have disclosed several means of which she would have approved. But as it so happens, and not surprisingly given the magnitude of the circumstances, Helen had hit upon one means that met with her overwhelming approval, and to that she gave her resounding consent upon leaving the well-house, dizzied and excited by newly created prospects that resulted from her "soul's sudden awakening." This deep change in Helen's life carries her forward to the cusp of a momentous attitude shift that occurs in showing *preference*; and so, the process of the action mode of wonder is as yet incomplete, for as Aquinas observed, "a choice still remains open after consent."

The image below represents *the fourth stage* of Helen's state of wonder in action mode described above. The what-to-do-wonder is the fourth of five basic attitudes that can be associated with five meanings of the word why. It is the fourth drive toward making sense of our experience, the occurrence of which we associate with the exemplary cause. The arrow below the boxes denotes the movement of this attitude shift.

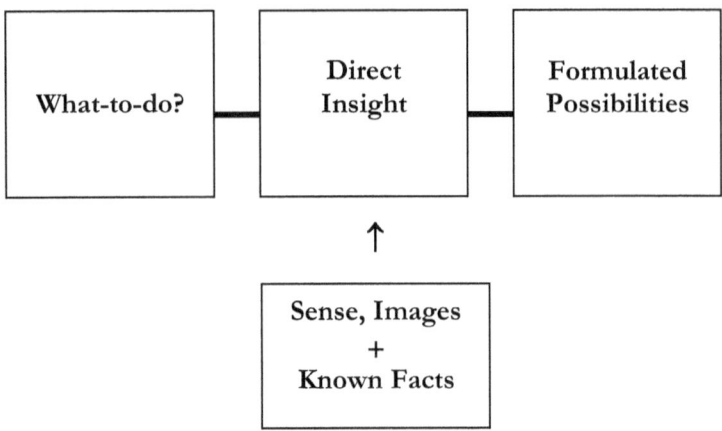

5. Is-it-to-be-done?

Because Helen had clearly formulated one possible means that overwhelmingly met with her approval, an achievement to which she gave her resounding consent, we arrive at *the fifth stage of wonder*, the recurrence of which emerges that day in seven-year-old Helen and surfaces at some point in our childhood selves. We draw further on Aquinas' empirical observations with which to bring our fifth core attitude into focus: "But if one alone meets with approval, then consent and choice coincide in point of fact, though they remain distinct meanings, for we think of consent as approval, and of choice as a preference."[46] And so what-to-do questions and answers (consent as approval) have their full home in this larger reaching of *is-to-do wonder* (choice as a preference). And Aquinas identifies the activity that involves our leap to preference or to choice. It is a leap that brings about a positive reality that otherwise would not have come about.

How does Helen reach the point of following through on what she plans to do? What goes on in her mind when she reaches for and arrives at a decision? Recall the eagerness Helen generates at the prospect of learning, and her renewed enthusiasm since the hand-touching of Annie has opened the world to her. This stance in Helen, no doubt, proves to be the catalyst for her spontaneous *fifth attitude shift* to *is-to-do questions*. Helen's search at this level is to affirm that her plan is *responsible*, *good*, *worthwhile*, of *value*. The is-to-do question asks: Is this plan worth putting into action?

At the fifth attitude shift, Helen finds herself spontaneously *weighing* and *evaluating the evidence* of her formulated plan. Her plan is *conditioned*: if it intelligently meets her needs it will be a good plan. "I learned a great many new words that day. I do not remember what they all were; but I do know that *mother*, *father*, *sister*, *teacher* were among them – words that were to make the world blossom for me, 'like Aaron's rod, with flowers.' It would have been difficult to find a happier child than I was as I lay in my crib at the close of that eventful day and lived over the joys it had brought me, and for the first time longed for a new day to come."[47] Still, Helen's deliberations on the value of her plan involve a rapid back and forth movement, a continuous interaction of senses and imagination: "I did nothing but explore with my hands and learn the name of every object that I touched."[48] But Helen's is-to-do questions do not end there. She is wondering about implications and consequences: by giving reasons (causes) for carrying out this plan. Why should I do this? "[T]he more I handled things and learned their names and uses, the more joyous and confident grew my sense of kinship with the rest of the world."[49] She also weighs the meaning of the plan for herself, its consequences in her life: "As my knowledge of things grew I felt more and more the delight of the world I was in."[50] Moreover, she must see her way clear in her commitment to act: "I am never discouraged by absence of good. I never can be argued into hopelessness."[51] As well, she must be secure that she is up to the task: "Doubt and mistrust are the mere panic of timid imagination, which the steadfast heart will conquer, and the large mind transcend."[52]

Her activity of thinking, questioning, of weighing and considering the evidence does not actually end until *the sixth attitude shift* in which she achieves an *is-insight*, upon which pivots her firm *decision*. Helen achieves an *is-insight* with "a prophetic vision of the good that would come of the undertaking."[53] For Helen, this insight grounds the reality where one possibility alone meets with approval, and consent and choice coincide in point of fact. Evidence for the judgment has been grasped, the judgment proceeds of necessity.

Consent and choice converge with *the seventh attitude shift* when Helen makes a firm decision about the value of language and its importance in her life; it is a convergence that we call "The Joy of Choice," a *judgment of value*, 'Yes! I will do it!' The judgment of value is actually two simultaneous, complementary judgments. The first judgment of value regards the *good-to-be-achieved*. Helen decides to do it because "To what is good I open the doors of my being, and jealously shut them against what is bad."[54] The second judgment of value regards *the satisfaction of that very judgment*. Helen decides to do it because "Such is the force of this beautiful and willful conviction, it carries itself in the face of all opposition."[55] She later recalls this great leap forward, that the means are, of necessity, worth the end:

> With the dropping of a little word from another's hand into mine, a slight flutter of the fingers, began the intelligence, the joy, the fullness of my life. Like Job, I feel as if a hand had made me, fashioned me together round about and molded my very soul.[56]

Helen's judgment of value blossoms into the fullness of two further momentous decisions that spring from this life-changing course of action. "Unprompted, Helen wrote on her tablet: "I wish to write about things I do not understand."[57] "From the beginning, Helen Keller was a writer…who found wholeness and salvation in words."[58] "[S]he painstakingly learned crude oral speech only several years later."[59] For as Helen recollects, "I resolved that I, too, would learn to speak."[60]

The process of Helen Keller's breakthrough to language is a process that moves in parallel lines to our infant/childhood selves. The five core attitudes are spontaneously in Helen and in our infant/childhood selves before, during and after the first sudden event of language learning and, as a result, subsequent events of language acquisition emerge in a recurrent series of shifts from babbling to talk. This activity of 'making sense', by way of understanding and using words, allows language users to choose to bring to fruition their potential for knowing and doing what is truly good.

The arrow below denotes the relationship between the what-to-do and is-to-do attitudes. Is-to-do wonder is the fifth of five basic attitudes that can be associated with five meanings of the word why. It is the fifth drive toward making sense of our experience, the occurrence of which we associate with the final cause.

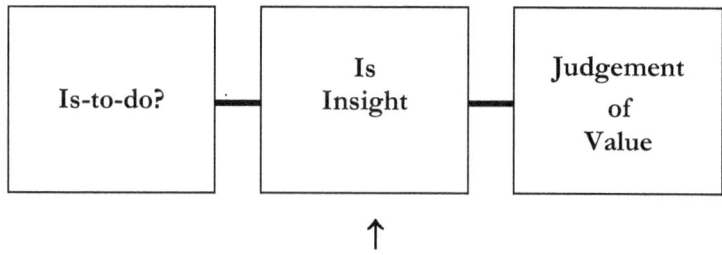

We draw our lengthy venture with Helen and our infant/childhood selves to a close. Thus far, we have an enlarged thematic identification of our five core attitudes as the basis for the grounding language universals. However, we have postponed formally naming these core psychological facts the grounding language universals. This identification takes place in Chapter 6, where the attitudes and achievements we have accumulated to this point will be assembled and further thematic considerations will be brought to bear. Only then can they be deemed necessary and sufficient with which to identify the language universals that ground generic linguistic performance.

---

[1] Concurrently, we are searching for the elements of core grammar.
[2] Op. cit., *BHT*, pp. 30-31. I take this opportunity to thank Philip McShane and Alessanda Drage for their generosity in granting me permission to reproduce freely from *BHT* and *TW*, respectively, throughout this and subsequent chapters.
[3] We are also in slow pursuit of an appreciation of five basic attitudes that can be associated with five meanings of the word why. In each core attitude there is a searching, a searcher, for regularity, for ruledness, for sense. See Chapter 3.
[4] Thus, our venture also reveals that the discovery of language universals is primarily the result of a self-search. Recalling the challenge posed in the Introduction, the discovery of the dynamics of one's five-leveled structure of wonder is, at the same time, a discovery of one's core self. This book is meant to encourage you, the reader and the language user, to gently discover the dynamics of core grammar by meeting yourself. For an introduction to a series

of elementary exercises with which to undertake that self-search, I would direct readers to the following three sources: op. cit., *ICT*, Section IV, op. cit., *BHT*, Chapters 1 and 2 and op. cit., *TW*, Chapters 3-7.

[5] Op. cit., *Verbum*, p. 41. Helen's ability to overcome the loss of two senses, most significantly her sight, gives weight to an advanced counter-cultural position on the status of seeing and the problem of correct understanding and the real. This issue has been named "the myth of the eyeballs." See op. cit., *ICT*, Chapter 19, op. cit., *Wealth*, Chapter 5, and op. cit., *Insight*, Chapter XIV.

[6] Helen Keller, *The Story of My Life*. New York: Doubleday, 1954, p. 35.

[7] Ibid.

[8] Joseph P. Lash, *Helen and Teacher*. Delacorte Press, New York, 1980, p. 51.

[9] Ibid., p. 256.

[10] The triple sequence and analysis of it is borrowed from op. cit., *BHT*, pp. 31-32, 34-37, 51-53, 55, and 73.

[11] Ibid., *Helen and Teacher*.

[12] This attitude, of course, is the "turn to the idea," a *Wendung zür idee* that dominated our attention in Chapters 2 and 3 and grounds later chapters.

[13] Op. cit., *Summa Theologiae*, Ia Q.84, a.7.

[14] Op. cit., *Helen and Teacher*.

[15] Ibid., *The Story of My Life*, p. 36.

[16] On this point, the research of Dr. Candace Pert is of great significance and relevance. She conceives of a human in terms of a "whole" organism. "Mind doesn't dominate body, it becomes body – body and mind are one. I see the process…throughout the whole organism, as evidence that the body is the actual outward manifestation, in physical space, of the mind…the body is inseparable from the mind." The direction of her research is in harmony with the assertions being made here. See Candace Pert, *Molecules and Emotion*, New York: Touchstone, 1997, p. 187. Also see Lonergan: "Study of the organism begins from the thing-for-us, from the organism as exhibited to our senses." Op. cit., *Insight*, p. 464 [489].

[17] Op. cit., *Verbum*, p. 40.

[18] Ibid.

[19] A distinction must be drawn here that will have great import in Chapter 7. It is important to note that in Helen, as well as in ourselves as infants during both our initial and subsequent struggles from babbling to talk, the achievement of our naming a word and attributing to it a meaning that is commonly accepted, results in the achievement of a nominal definition, that of naming things in relation to ourselves, the mastery of which is sufficient for us to function in the practical world of descriptive common sense. (In Chapter 7, we give Lonergan's clarification of how the occurrence of insight into language works by distinguishing between a nominal and an explanatory definition, op. cit., *Insight*, p. 11 [36].) Helen is in the wondrous state of *raising herself up* to a nominal definition of her first word. The initial mastery of language is a complex rite of passage for all humans, the achievement of which places humans in the intelligible world of meaning in which the capacity and need to

elevate talk to the level of an explanatory definition then becomes the core drive. We are talking here about the human drive toward a more difficult rite of passage, the horizon of scientific thinking identified in Chapter 2 by Aristotle. The expression "elevate" is found in Patrick H. Byrne, *Analysis and Science in Aristotle*. State University of New York Press, 1997. See "To Reduce or to Elevate (Anagein)?", pp. 23-27. I note here that the expression relates to Byrne's work on the meaning of *analysis*. It occurs at the conclusion of that analysis in his discussion of a somewhat parallel word, *anagein*. It is important to notice that Byrne goes against a solid tradition that would relate that word to *reduction*, and makes the case for a richer Aristotelian meaning surrounding the general sense of *raising up*: water by heat, an audience by rhetoric and, significantly, potency to act. The basic elements of this elevated talk are introduced in Chapters 2 and 3. Further refinements with respect to potency and act can be found in op. cit. *Insight*, p. 651 [674] on "Causality". "The basic division is between external and internal causes. Internal causes are the central and conjugate potency, form, and act..."

[20] Op. cit., *Verbum*, pp. 42. Obviously, this reinforces Lonergan's point above about the need for sense experience: "a person without sense perception would never learn anything or understand anything."

[21] The key passage is ibid., pp. 41-42. The introduction of the frontispiece of the book *Insight* has a quotation from Aristotle (*De Anima*, III, 7) that includes the key word *phantasmasi*, the key doctrine of Aquinas and Lonergan, "insight into phantasm."

[22] Ibid., 38. Of course, prolonged self-attention would be needed to reach the level of refinement described by Lonergan here about the tricky relationship between phantasm and insight: "The act of intellect with respect to phantasm is an insight... insight is to phantasm as form is to matter; but in that proportion, form is related to prime matter, but insight is related to sensible qualities; strictly, then, it is not true that insight is grasp of form; rather, insight is the grasp of the object in an inward aspect such that the mind, pivoting on the insight, is able to conceive, not without labor, the...concepts of form and matter."

[23] For the many references to inner word in Aquinas one might begin with Lonergan's seven elements in "The General Notion of the Inner Word," ibid., pp. 13-24. Lonergan notes the influence of Aristotle in Aquinas' thought: "Four other works of recognized standing divide inner words into the two classes of definitions and judgments, and three of these recall the parallel of the Aristotelian twofold operation of the mind." Lonergan thus footnotes this statement with: *De veritate*, q. 4, a. 2 c.; q. 3., a. 2 c.; *De potentia*, q. 8, a. 1 c.; q. 9, a. 5 c.; *Quaestiones quodlibetales*, 5, a. 9 c.; *Super Ioannem*, c. 1, lect. 1., ibid., p. 17.

[24] In this chapter I draw heavily on ibid. For a full account for the meaning of is-questions see Chapter 2, "Verbum: Reflection and Judgement," pp. 60-105.

[25] Ibid., pp. 60-61.

[26] Quid sit? [What is it?] An sit? [Is it so?]

[27] Op. cit., *Helen and Teacher*, pp. 256-7.

[28] Op. cit., *The Story of My Life*.
[29] Op. cit., *Thinking Woman*, pp. 65-66. I draw the reader's attention to further refinements of Lonergan on the is-attitude that are beyond the elementary scope of this chapter. See *Insight*, Chapter IX, especially "6. Probable Judgments," pp. 299-304 [324-29].
[30] It is important to note at this stage that the three core attitudes we have identified so far, taken together, are the dynamic underpinning for the activities of "syllogizing," and "logic." These activities have been commonly mistaken to mean the laws of "reason." I cannot enlarge on that topic here, except to quote Lonergan's caution in *Insight*: "A little learning is a dangerous thing, and the adage has, perhaps, its most abundant illustrations from the application of logic.... A familiarity with the elements of logic can be obtained by a very modest effort and in a very short time. Until one has made notable progress in cognitional analysis [knowledge of our core dynamics of wonder], one is constantly tempted to mistake the rules of logic for the laws of thought." (*Insight*, p. 573 [595-96]) With that in mind, I take this opportunity, then, to direct the reader to luminous introductions to "syllogizing" and "logic" in op. cit., *BHT*, Chapter 2, "How Language: Works?," pp. 57-65 and op. cit., *ICT*, Chapter 26, "Fallacies," pp. 100-104 and Chapter 27, "The Function of Logic," pp. 104-108. For advanced treatment, see Bernard Lonergan, "The Form of Inference," *Collection (CWL 4)*, University of Toronto Press, 1988, Chapter 1.
[31] Op. cit., *The Story of My Life*, p. 25. I include the context of that quote here as Helen compares her language acquisition to those children who hear: "I had now the key to all language, and I was eager to learn to use it. Children who hear acquire language without any particular effort; the words that fall from others' lips they catch on the wing, as it were, delightedly, while the little deaf child must trap them by a slow and often painful process."
[32] The illustration given here of the action mode of wonder is very elementary. Again, I appeal to the reader to grasp that the purpose of our venture into its discovery necessarily involves a self-search, to discover the dynamics of one's five-leveled structure of wonder is, at the same time, a discovery of one's core self. This book is meant to encourage you, the language user, to gently discover the dynamics of core grammar by meeting yourself. Reading through this section can be a deceptively easy exercise. However, if the reader seriously takes up the challenge to understand it better, many more complexities will emerge in diagnosing the patterns of minding that are involved. This relates to the elementary exercises suggested at the beginning of this chapter, as well as in Chapter 8.
[33] Helen recalls, "Gradually from naming an object we advance step by step until we have traversed the vast distance between our first stammered syllable and the sweep of thought in a line of Shakespeare." Op. cit., *The Story of My Life*, p. 25.
[34] Op. cit., *Summa Theologiae*, Ia Iiae. Q.15, a. 3. According to Aquinas, this process occurs in a curious mixed sequence of twelve basic steps. I cannot

enlarge here on this achievement of Aquinas. He wrote it up in a central section of the *Summa Theologiae* (Q. 6-17 of the beginning of the second part). We briefly mention "consent" above. He deals with its complexities in Q. 15. It took him fifty pages of two-column Latin that comes out in translation to one hundred pages.

[35] Op. cit., *The Story of My Life*, p. 39.
[36] Helen Keller, *The World I Live In*. The New York Review of Books, 2003, p. 128-29.
[37] Op. cit., *The Story of My Life*, p. 20
[38] Op cit., *Helen and Teacher*, 257.
[39] Op. cit., *The Story of My Life*, 20.
[40] Ibid., p. 25.
[41] Op. cit., *The World I Live In*, p. 128.
[42] Op. cit., *The Story of My Life*, p. 25.
[43] Ibid., p. 33.
[44] Ibid., p. 20.
[45] Op. cit., *Summa Theologiae*.
[46] Op. cit., *Summa Theologiae*, Ia Iiae. Q.15, a. 3. 17 of the beginning of the second part.
[47] Op. cit., *The Story of My Life*, p. 20.
[48] Ibid., p. 21.
[49] Ibid.
[50] Ibid.
[51] Op. cit., *The World I Live In*, pp. 130-1. I would suggest this passage and others that follow, written in retrospect by an older, more articulate Helen, accurately express the strength of character of the younger, resolute Helen at the time of these events.
[52] Ibid.
[53] Op. cit., *The Story of My Life*, p. 59.
[54] Op. cit., *The World I Live In*, pp. 130-1.
[55] Ibid.
[56] Ibid., p. 10.
[57] Ibid., p. x.
[58] Ibid., p. ix.
[59] Op. cit., *The Story of My Life*, p. ix.
[60] Ibid., p. 48.

5

LANGUAGE UNIVERSALS IN THE INDO-EUROPEAN BRANCH

This chapter brings the previous chapters together to provide a classification of attitudes and achievements that are necessary and sufficient with which to identify language universals, and as a result, to ground generic linguistic performance in the Aryan Branch of the Indo-European tradition.[1]

Mediated by the empirically verified universal attitudes and achievements of his adventurous predecessors, Aristotle and Aquinas, Lonergan went on to thematize their terms and relations. These terms and relations bore fruit in a cognitional theory[2] that underpins language universals in Arjuna, Helen Keller and ourselves, the expressions of which are grounded by a desire to have an idea, or to have the facts of some matter, or to reach a plan for the day, or for life, or to figure out which way to go, the utterance of which dawns with a first word and ushers forth, in a variety of tongues, our core humanity.[3] So it is that all human tongues, in moving from babbling to talk, express these language universals, directed in the same ways, regardless of one's sex or when or where one was born or lives, whether it be in an ancient village or a modern city. As such, language universals may be drawn from

(1) the empirically attentive subject as language user who experiences sensory data
(2) the intelligently inquiring subject as language user who raises the question, "what is it? and "why is it so?"
(3) the critically reflecting subject as language user who raises the question, "is it so?"
(4) the responsibly deliberating subject as language user who raises the question "what is to be done?"
(5) the responsibly deliberating subject as language user who raises the question "is it to be done?"[4]

Lonergan terms the achievement of knowledge of these

operations to be "self-knowledge."⁵ In other words, the language user's self-knowledge illuminates these different operations and their relations to one another. For Lonergan, then, acts of understanding in the language user have the triple role of responding to inquiry, grasping intelligible form in sensible representations, and grounding the formation of concepts. What promotes the levels from sensible to intellectual consciousness in the subject as language user is the desire to understand, the intention of intelligibility.⁶ What next promotes the levels from intellectual to rational consciousness, is a fuller unfolding of the same intention: for the language user's desire to understand, once understanding is reached, becomes the desire to understand correctly; in other words, the language user's intention of intelligibility, once an intelligible is reached, becomes the intention of the right intelligible, of the true and, through truth, of reality. Finally, the language user's intention of the intelligible, the true, the real, becomes also the intention of the good, the question of value, of what is worthwhile.⁷ In brief, the language user's consciousness operates integrally and dynamically on five levels: experience, understanding, and judging to arrive at a knowledge of fact with which to ground possible courses of action for choice. The activity immediately related to this process we have identified as language universals is questioning, while other activities such as sensing and imagining, understanding, judging, and deciding are related mediately to the process inasmuch as they supply the means of answering questions, of reaching the goal intended by questioning.

The language universals gleaned from the empirical investigations originally quarried by Aristotle, enlarged and refined by Aquinas, and then thematized by Lonergan, may be formally categorized thus:

> Expressions of wonder: The Dynamics of Knowing
> Core Invariant Questions: What is it? → Is it so?
>
> Expressions of wonder: The Dynamics of Doing
> Core Invariant Questions: What is to be done? → Is it to be done?

We now have two categories of language universals: "The Dynamics of Knowing," and "The Dynamics of Doing."[8] These two categories are recast into two images below.[9] These two images furnish a classification of attitudes and achievements that are, in fact, necessary and sufficient with which to ground generic linguistic performance in the Aryan Branch of the Indo-European tradition, and indeed, in any tongue.

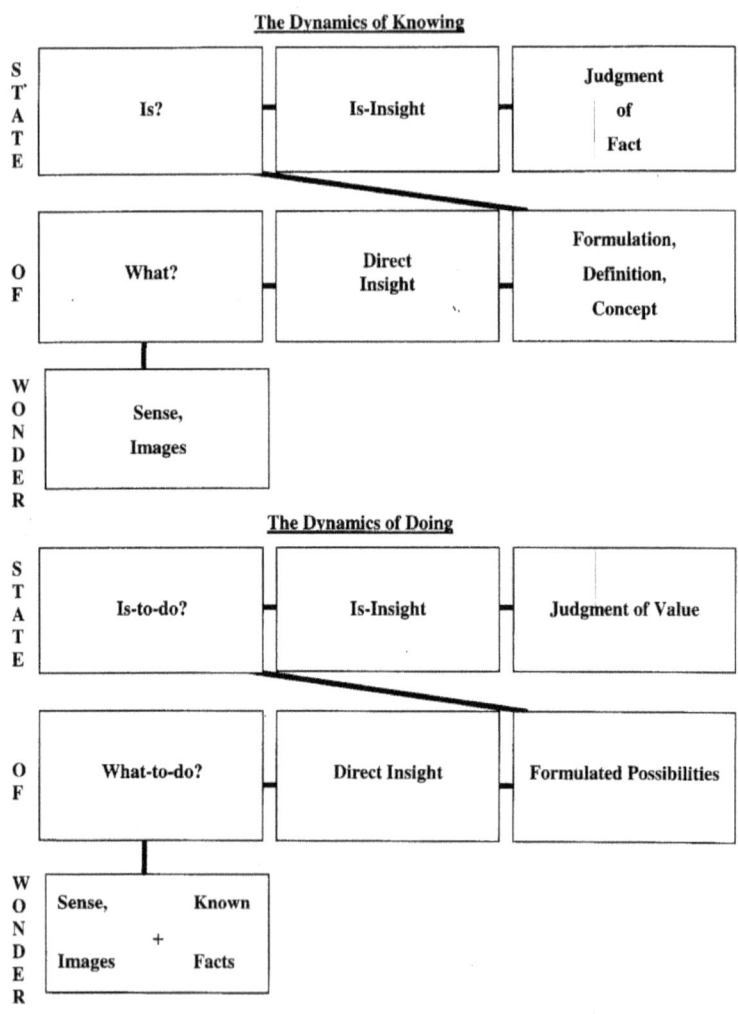

Below, I focus on raw data taken from the Aryan Branch within the Indo-European tradition. The tables below show empirical evidence of language universals[10] in ancient Sanskrit,[11] as well as in its direct descendant, modern Hindi.[12]

The Dynamics of Knowing What?

Ancient Sanskrit	Modern Hindi
kutah = from what?	*kab ?* = when?
kim-artham = from what cause?	*kaun ?* = who?
hetu = ground for, cause	*kis ?* = which?
prcchâti = he asks	*kahan ?* = where?
katham = how?	*kaise ?* = how?
kah (kim) = what?	*kitna ?* = how much?
tatah kim = what of it?	*kitne ?* = how many?
yada = when?	*kab tak ?* = how long?
kva = where?	*kya ?* = what?
kutah = where from?	*kuchh bhi* = whatever
kah = which?	*jahan kahin* = wherever
kah = who/whom?	*kyun ?* = why?
kim = why?	*chunki, isliye ki* = because
kim vadati? = what is he saying?	*jaise taise* = somehow or other
kim socasi? = why do you grieve?	*kahin na kahin* = somewhere or other
avagacchati = he understands	*utna* = so much, so many
apy avagacchasi = do you understand?	*kuchh* = something
kutuhalam = curiosity	*yeh lafz kya hai?* = what is this word?
ativa me kautukam vartate = I am feeling intensely curious	

Is?

Ancient Sanskrit	Modern Hindi
kim and *api* = yes; expect a yes or no answer *na or a:* = no *asti etat* = this is true, that is so *kascit* = certain *as, bhu* = be *bhuta* = having become, being *tarhi* = I infer that *jna; vid; ava+gam* = know *vikalpah* = uncertainty *satya* = true *asti; ayam; asau* = there is *really* = satyam *asti* = be, exist *nimitta:bhuta* = being the cause *ava+gam* = realize *kim tatra gacchati?* = is he going there? (or why is he going there?) *api jayati?* = is he winning? *api viditam etat devasya?* = Is this known to Your Majesty?	*han* = yes *nahin* = no *hona* = to be *zarur; beshak* = surely *sach* = much truly *ho na ho, beshak* = undoubtedly *Yeh sach hai.* = It is the truth. *Tum nahin jante?* = Don't you know? *Kya yeh lafz asan hain* = are the words easy? *Main nahin janta hun* or *mujhe nahin malum hai* = I do not know

The Dynamics of Doing

What-to-do?

Ancient Sanskrit	Modern Hindi
kr, karoti = do, make	*karana, pura karana* = do
kim kurmah? = What shall we do?	*Kya ap mujhko yeh karne denge?* = Will you allow me to do it?
kriya = action	
anutisthati, anusthita = carry out, perform, act	*Ap iskokaise karte hain?* = how do you do this?
karin = doing	*Kya ap hamen bataenge ki is mamlemen ham ap ke liye kya kar sakte hain?* = Will you let us know what we can do for you in this matter?
kurvanti = do (from kRi)	
kurvantu = may do	

Is-to-do?

Ancient Sanskrit	Modern Hindi
krtin = having something done *akari* = was done *purva:krta* or *krta:purva* = previously done, already done *akaarya* = what ought not to be done *akaarye* = and what ought not to be done *kartavya* = should be done *kartavya* = prescribed duty *kartavyaani* = should be done as duty *karmaaNi* = deeds	*Agar yeh karna hai, to fauran karo* = If it is to be done, do it at once. *Main janta hun ki mujhe kya karna hai* = I know what I have to do. *Kisi na kisi ko yeh karna chahiye* = Someone must do it. *Ab yeh kara* = do it now. *Main tumko yeh karne deta hun.* = I allow you to do it. *Ham usko nahin kar sakte* = we can not do it *Kya tum mere liye yeh kar doge?* = Will you do it for me? *Jaisa main tumhen kahun vaisa karo.* = Do as I tell you.

These tables show empirical evidence of language universals in the language of ancient Sanskrit, and its direct descendant, modern Hindi. Moreover, as generic categories, the language universals identified in this chapter denote a classification of attitudes and achievements that are, in fact, necessary and sufficient with which to ground generic linguistic performance. Again, briefly, language universals express a generic process that operates integrally and dynamically on five levels: sense and image (experience), what-questions (understanding), and is-questions (judging) so as to arrive at knowledge of fact. Knowledge of fact, sense and image then combine to ground what-to-do questions (possible courses of action) and is-to-do-questions (the good-to-be achieved and the satisfaction of that very judgment).

In Chapter 6 I provide more empirical evidence of language universals from a group of dominant branches in the linguistic tree. Our attention turns there to the Semitic, African, Asian, Nordic, and Teutonic languages.

---

[1] I note immediately that the mode of procedure in Chapters 5 and 6 runs in parallel lines to the empirical procedure undertaken in Chapters 1 and 3. Its purpose is to produce the data of language universals across a spectrum of

dominant languages. The source of this data in this and the next chapter is drawn from an assortment of dictionaries and grammar texts.

[2] A fiercely compact article by Lonergan called "Cognitional Structure" can be found in *Introducing the Thought of Bernard Lonergan*, Philip McShane (ed.), London: Darton, Longman & Todd, 1973. Even though I reproduce a small measure of that compactness here, equally important is the suggestion to soak up Philip McShane's cautionary introduction to the three articles in the book.

[3] Again, I defer further detail of Lonergan's very compact thematization with an appeal to the reader to undertake a prolonged Proustian reading of, and reflection on, "Cognitional Structure," the difficult, but precise intussception of which very gradually "brings us to the epistemological theorem, namely, that knowing in the proper sense is intrinsically objective, that objectivity is the intrinsic relation of knowing to being, and that being and reality are identical." (*Ibid.*, p. 22) In addition, since we have already introduced the isomorphism of the dynamics of knowing and the dynamics of doing to a series of distinct causes directed toward specific goals, I reproduce a suggestive pointing to that relationship from that very heavy article: "Accordingly, the dynamic structure of human knowing [and doing] intends being. That intention is unrestricted, for there is nothing that we cannot at least question. The same intention is comprehensive, for questioning probes every aspect of everything; its ultimate goal is the universe in its full concreteness. Being in that sense is identical with reality: as apart from being there is nothing, so apart from reality there is nothing; as being embraces the concrete totality of everything, so too does reality." (*Ibid.*)

[4] The generic categories as presented here are also drawn from another compendious article in Bernard Lonergan, *The Subject*, Marquette University Press, 1968, pp. 7-8. [subsequently referred to as *Subject*] Please note I have added the term "language user" to Lonergan's term "subject," to reinforce the core identity between the speaker and the spoken.

[5] Op. cit., "Cognitional Structure," p. 19. "Self-knowledge is the reduplicated structure: it is experience, understanding, and judging with respect to experience, understanding, [judging and deciding]."

[6] Ibid., pp. 7-8.

[7] Ibid, p. 23.

[8] The reader will notice that I have assembled the different stages of the two processes, introduced in Chapter 4, into a complete image of each.

[9] These diagrams, with some further refinements, appear in Bernard Lonergan, *Phenomenology and Logic* (*CWL 18*), University of Toronto Press, 2001. See "Appendix A Two Diagrams," pp. 319-323.

[10] I also supplement the language universals with the data of related question patterns and statement attitudes underpinned by language universals: What might that be? Who? Where? When? Which? How? be, being, because, cause, concern, decide, define, definition, decision, do, good, judge, know, reason, thing, understand, value.

[11] Michael Coulson, *Sanskrit*. London: Hodder and Stoughton, 1992. Raw data of ancient Sanskrit has been drawn exclusively from this book.
[12] *Hindustani in Three Months*. New Delhi: Vikas Publishing House, 1993. Raw data of Hindustani has been drawn exclusively from this book.

6

LANGUAGE UNIVERSALS IN THE DOMINANT BRANCHES OF THE LINGUISTIC TREE

We now shift to a cross-section of the dominant branches of the linguistic tree.[1] Once again, I present empirical evidence of language universals with raw data taken from Semitic, African, Asian, Nordic, and Teutonic branches. In this cross-section of tongues, I supplement the data in each section with suggestive observations by scholars in each language who note the manner of intonation associated with the spontaneity of asking questions. Their comments reveal both parallel and distinctive events in intonation, as well as mood, which accompany the universal dynamics of human wonder.

1. Empirical Evidence in the Semitic Branch: Arabic

In *Modern Arabic Prose*, Cantarino writes:

> Arabic does not require any special word order or particle in order to express a question: rather, the emphasis or the intonation by itself can change a statement into a question. Usually, however, a question will be introduced by a special element that will indicate the interrogative character of the expression. The grammatically appropriate interrogative element will be used according to the purpose of the question.[2]

The Dynamics of Knowing What?[3]

fahima to understand	فهم: أُدرك	bä'it *motive, cause*	باعث
istifhäm *inquiry, act of inquiring*	إستفهام	shai *thing, matter*	شيئى: أمر

مَا, as the counterpart of مَنْ, asks **for identification of things in a specific or generic way**:

مَا هِيَ أَشْهَرُ ٱلثَّقَافَاتِ فِى ذٰلِكَ ٱلْعَصْرِ؟	What was the most famous culture of that period? Amin duh. I, 170, 7
مَا هُوَ ٱلشَّرْطُ؟	What is the condition? Hak. sul. 31, 9
مَا ٱلَّذِى حَيَّرَكُمْ؟	What is it that confuses you? Amin (Zy.) 7, 8

and also for a **definition**, in which case مَا can refer to persons as well as to things:

مَا مَعْنَى هٰذَا ٱلْكَلَامِ؟	What does this word mean? Hus. ayy. II, 21, 1
مَا هُوَ ٱلْأَدَبُ ٱلْعَرَبِيُّ ٱلْقَدِيمُ؟ هُوَ أَدَبٌ كَانَ ـ	What is ancient Arabic literature? It is a literature which was.... Musa adab. 6, 1
مَا هِيَ فَلْسَفَتُكَ ٱلْأَدَبِيَّةُ وَٱلْإِجْتِمَاعِيَّةُ؟	What is your cultural and social philosophy? Musa adab. 121, 4

إِذًا مَا هُوَ ٱلرَّجُلُ ٱلْإِنْفِرَادِىُّ؟	Then what is an individualist? Musa adab. 76, 8
إِذًا مَا هُوَ ٱلنَّابِغَةُ؟	Then what is a famous man? Musa adab. 20, 5

It is a characteristic of مَا that it can be used for questions about **any kind of qualifications** or **circumstances** involved in the statement regarding persons as well as things:

مَا لَكَ؟	What is the matter with you? Hai. sir. 111, 1
مَا ٱسْمُكَ؟	What is your name? Gibr. I, 80, 16
مَا بَالُكَ وَجَمَسْتَ؟	Why are you so silent? Hak. (Br.) 40, 1

It may also take on the **function of an adverbial accusative** (see page 142):

مَا دَخَلَ ٱلشَّرَفُ فِى ٱلْأَدَبِ؟	What has honor to do with culture? [How is honor included in culture?] Musa adab. 47, 14, (46, 8)
مَاذَا يُهِمُّنَا أَيْنَ تَعِيشُ ٱلْأَكْثَرِيَّةُ؟	Why should we be interested in where the majority lives? Jabr. (Br.) 69, 20

arafa
to know

Is?

عرف ـ يعرِف

§ 40 QUESTIONS ABOUT THE VALIDITY OF THE STATEMENT

This category expresses the idea as uncertain, and asks about its truth, thus seeking an affirmative or negative answer.

No special word order or special particle is required to show the interrogative character of sentences in this category.[39] It is expressed only by the intonation and, in modern printing, by the question mark:

وَهِيَ فِى ٱلدَّارِ؟	Is she in the house? Raf. wah. I, 136, 16
حَيَاتِى فِى خَطَرٍ؟	Is my life in danger? Hak. sheh. 15, 15
إِبْنَتِى نَجِيَه عَادَتْ؟	Has my daughter, Najiya, come back? Tai. (Zy.) 34, 6
وَتَعْلَمُ ذٰلِكَ؟	and do you know that? Hus. 'ala. II, 168, 21
لَا أَحَدَ يَدْرِى؟	Nobody knows? Hak. sheh. 11, 4
أَكَلْتَ دَبْسَاً؟	Did you eat honey? Hus. ayy. I, 20, 14
وَلَا بُدَّ مِن هٰذَا؟ قَالَ لَا بُدَّ	"Is there no way out of this?" He answered, "No." Raf. wah. I, 176, 18

---

[39] تَرَى؟, "do you think...?" used in interrogative constructions is derived from the verb رَأَى, "to see," hence, "to think." تَرَى has also always been used in the passive voice (تُرَى). (See Brock., *Grund.*, II, p. 189; Fleischer, *Beitr.*, VI, p. 103.)

تَرَى and تُرَى have completely become particles which emphasize the doubt raised by the question. They no longer belong to the structure of the interrogative sentence having, rather, an interjectional character; they can be used preceding, following, or even in the middle of the sentence. تُرَى is frequently preceded by the particle يَا:

The Dynamics of Doing

What-to-do?

fa'la
to do, perform

فعل - يفعل

رَغِبَ أَنْ يَفْعَلَ شَيْئًا أَيًّا كَانَ — He longed to do something, whatever it might be. Mah. qah. 127, 1

Is-to-do?

فَيَقُولُ لَكَ «نَعَمْ سَأَفْعَلُ هٰذَا» — He will answer you, "Yes, I'll do that." Hus. ayy. I, 30, 15

iktāra   إختار : انتخب
to choose

2. Empirical Evidence in the African Branch: Swahili

In *African Voices*, Webb and Kembo-Sure note: "The Niger-Congo languages form the largest language family in sub-Saharan Africa…A sub-group of these languages [is] known as the Bantu languages."[4] Welmers remarks in *African Language Structures* that "Swahili is unmistakably a Bantu language. No significant features of Arabic, English, or other foreign grammatical structures have crept into Swahili."[5] According to Wilson:

> [I]n Swahili…there is no change whatsoever in the formation of a question from a statement. When writing a question…the only clue that it is a question is the question mark. But in speech, the intonation is quite changed. In a statement, the voice is kept on a monotone until the last syllable or so, when it then lowers. But in a question, the voice is used at a slightly higher level than normal, and the last two or three syllables are spoken on an even higher pitch, with the slight drop for the final syllable.[6]

The Dynamics of Knowing

What?

Ku-uliza = question[7]
Ku-fahamu = to understand
Kwa nini? = Why? (For what?)
Gani? = What sort? Which kind of? Which?
Habari gani? = What is the news?[8]
Jinsi kilivyo ajabu. = What a wonderful thing!
Kwa sababu(ya) = because
Kuna nini? = What is there? What is the matter? (Loogman 363)
Sababu nini? (or better: *Sababu gani*) = What for? For what reason? With what intention? (Loogman 363)
Maana yake nini? = What is the meaning of this? (Loogman 363)

Is?

Ndiyo = Yes. (Loogman 235)
Siyo = No. (Loogman 235)
Hivo? = Is that so? (Loogman 95)
Yaweza kuwa ya kweli = this may be true. (Loogman 95)
Kweli = It is true. (Loogman 411)
Ku-wa = to be
Ku-jua = to know

The Dynamics of Doing

What-to-do?

Ku-fanya = to do
Itafaa nini? = What is it good for? (Loogman 363)
Nitakayefanya = I who shall do. (Wilson 165)

Is-to-do?

Sikuwa nimefanya = I had not done (Wilson 227)
Tafadhali ufanye, nataka sana ufanye = Do do it.
Husu = concern

3. Empirical Evidence in the Asian Branch: Cantonese

With respect to intonation in Cantonese, Po-fei Huang observes

> the mood of the speaker will often influence the pitch relationships of his tones; when excited, for instance, he may extend the pitch range of his voice so that the distance between higher and lower tones becomes greater and the rising and falling tones rise and fall farther than usual. Besides this, even in normal, unexcited speech the individual will show slight variations in the pitch-levels or end-points of his tones.[9]

The Dynamics of Knowing

What?

Mihng, mihng-baahk = understand (get the meaning of) (Huang 324)
Neih mihng-baahk meih a? = Do you understand now? (Huang 324)
Ngoh mh-mihng(-baahk) neih ge yi-si = I don't understand what you mean? (Huang 324)
Mat-yeh, me-yeh = What? (Huang 342)
Jouh-mat-yeh, waih-mat-sih, dim-gaai = Why?
Jouh mat-yeh a? = What's the matter? (Huang 342)
Mat-yeh wa = What do you mean? (Huang 342)
Gam haih mat-yeh yi si a? / *Gam haih dim-gaai a?* = What does that mean? (Huang 342)
Go-go haih mat-yeh a? = What is that? (Huang 342)
Ni-go giu-jouh mat-yeh a? = What is this called? (Huang 342)
Dim-gaai a? = What is the meaning of it? (Huang 342)
Yan-waih, yan-waih…so-yih = because (Huang 27)
Yuhn-yan, yuhn-gu = cause (reason) (Huang 41)
Gahn-yan = the immediate cause (Huang 41)
Yuhn-yan = the underlying cause (Huang 41)

Is?

Jan = true (factual) (Huang 319)
Haih-mh-haih jan ga? = Is it true? (Huang 319)
Haih-mh-haih = Is it true that…? (Huang 319)
Dung-dak = judge (understand) (Huang 136)
Ji-dou = know (have knowledge about) (Huang 140)

Keuih ji mh-ji a? = Does he know? (Huang 140)
Waahk-je = That may be true (possibly will) (Huang 156)

The Dynamics of Doing

What-to-do?

Kyut-dihng = decide (Huang 62)
Dim-syun a? = What shall we do? (Huang 343)
Yauh mat hou-chyuh a? = What's the good of it? (Huang 343)
Keuih jouh gan mat-yeh a? = What is he doing? (Huang 342)
Jouh-hou-sih = do good (Huang 70)

Is-to-do?

Kyut-dihng = decide about (Huang 136)
Haih mh-haih gam jouh a? = Is this the right way to do it? (Huang 70)
Neih gam jouh mh-ngaam = You can't do it that way. (Huang 70)
Keuih wuih mh-wuih jing a? = Does he know how to do it? (Huang 70)

4. Empirical Evidence in the Nordic Branch: Swedish

Ahrenberg states "the investigations [of interrogatives] that have been undertaken in…Swedish suggest the following features are significant: overall higher pitch, overall frequency rise, wider pitch interval in connection with focus, compression of prefocal and postfocal pitch contours, terminal rise."[10]

The Dynamics of Knowing

What?

Orsaksmassig = causal (69)[11]
Kausalitet, orsakssammanhang = causality (69)
Fororsakande = causation (69)
Varfor fragar du det? = Why do you ask? (Ahrenberg 7)
Vad ar det me dig? = What's the matter…? (Ahrenberg 95)
Vada? = What do you mean? (Ahrenberg 128)
Hurda? = How do you mean? (Ahrenberg 128)
…*Och da undrar jag, varfor kommer man inte till samma resultat, nar man anda utgar fran samma siffror?* = …and then I wonder, why don't you come to the same conclusions, when you start with the same figures? (Ahrenberg 204)

Is?

Ja = Yes (Ahrenberg 34) *Nej* = No (Ahrenberg 34)
Det ar. = That is. (Ahrenberg 124)
Vet du var = Do you know? (Ahrenberg 71)
Det vet jag inte. = I don't know. (Ahrenberg 122)
Det ar inte sant att jorden ar platt. = It is not true that the earth is flat. (Ahrenberg 158)
Korpar ar svarta. = Ravens are black. (Ahrenberg 162)

The Dynamics of Doing

What-to-do?

Avgora, bestamma, besluta, fatta beslut om, faststalla, valja = decide, choose (Ahrenberg 205)
Vad gora? = What to do? (Ahrenberg 183)
Varfor gor du sa dar? = Why do you do that? (Ahrenberg 114)
Nu planerar jag vad gora nasta termin. = Now I'm planning what to do next term. (Ahrenberg 121)

Is-to-do?

Det gar inte = It can't be done. (129)
Bedoma, uppskatta, berakna = evaluate (Ahrenberg 214)

5. Empirical Evidence in the Teutonic Branch: German

The following data demonstrates how German intonation reflects the correlation between sentence mood and intonation:

a. Sentence type and speech acts
In formal speech, a distinction is, as noted above, generally made between three kinds of terminal or nuclear tone which characterise different speech acts: the falling terminal, typically associated with assertions; *the rising terminal, typically associated with yes/no questions*; and the mid-level terminal, typically called "progredient" or *weiterweisend*, i.e. continuative. In spontaneous speech, however, the mid-level progredient appears to be rare, except in stylised contexts, and *rising nuclei are used for a range of functions, from progredience to questions, but may also have connotations of deference, politeness, or uncertainty*...A range of interrelations between syntactic mood and speech act type is shown.[12]

The Dynamics of Knowing What?[13]

fragen = to ask oneself / wonder
sinnvoll = making sense / sensible
bedeuten = to mean / signify
glauben = to believe / think
überlegen = to think / consider / ponder
verstehen = to understand
die Theorie(en) = theory
grundsätzlich = in principle
sagen = to say / mean
bezweifeln = to doubt / question
unbedingt = necessarily
verallgemeinern = to generalize
dieLösung(en) = solution
das Problem(e) = problem
Wie soll ich das sagen? How shall I say this?
Was wollen Sie damit sagen? What do you mean by this?
Das sagt gar nichts. That doesn't mean anything…
Ich finde, die Lösung des Problems lieght in… I think the solution to the problem lies in…
Das wahre Problem
scheint mir ganz woanders zu liegen… The real problem seems to lie elsewhere.

Is?

Ich bin mir ganz sicher, daß… = I am completely certain that…
bestimmt = certainly
Das Weiß ich ganz bestimmt. I know that for sure.
stimmen = to be true
Das stimmt schon… That is true…
doch = yes
wahr = true
Das ist gar nicht wahr! That's not true at all!
falsch = wrong / false
gewiß = certainly
nein = no
unmöglich = impossible

Das gibt es doch nicht! <informal> = But that can't (possibly) be!
es mag wohl sein = it may well be
Glauben Sie wirklich? Do you really think so?
Ja? = Yes? / Really?
Weiß nicht. Don't know.

The Dynamics of Doing

What-to-do?

wie? corresponds to "how," and is synonymous with the phrase *auf welche Weise?* "in what way?" Thus, *wie heizt man die Wohnung?* "how is the flat heated?" (lit. "how does one heat...?), *wie unterscheidet man...?* "how does one distinguish...?", *wie spricht er deutch?* "how does he speak German?"
womit kann ich dienen? = What can I do for you?

Is-to-do?

so macht man es = it is done in that way or that's how it is done
etwas gut finden = to find / consider something (to be) good
sich lohnen = to be worthwhile / worth it

It is my hope that the evidence presented thus far will raise at least a minimal suspicion that the common patterns of quest in each language are more than a matter of coincidence. Whether or not one is convinced by the case presented in Chapters 1 to 6, the reader is reminded of the admonition made in the Introduction about the language user's curiosity regarding the data of his/her own quest. And so you may recall that the symbol "?" objectifies what Aristotle claims is a beginning, what Aquinas claims "[w]e can all experience in ourselves" and what Lonergan claims is the "effective emergence of wonder, of the desire to understand." The philosophers' agreement in principle on this fundamental point about wonder is arrived at "on the basis of empirical observation."

Now the fundamental point, as well as the problem, for you the language user, is to find a credible way either to agree or to disagree with them in principle. How? On the basis of empirical observation, by doing what they did, by attending to your own personal experience of wonder, by noticing how that experience is expressed in your spontaneous use of language and reflecting on what that experience means. Ask yourself: am I a specimen of what Aristotle, Aquinas and Lonergan are talking about? And does asking yourself this question, in your own words, provide you with some compelling evidence that would enable you either to agree or to disagree? Moreover, serious self-attentive puzzling over the symbol "?" would open up a fresh and novel way of how to read and how to reflect, not only on this claim, but also on any claim, including the claim that you have more than animal sensibility: for you have an undefined senseAbility.

The deeper problem, of course, is this kind of reading is virtually absent in every aspect of language studies. In the next chapter, I pursue this problem further by drawing attention to a regrettable tradition of reading, the dominance of which has systematically contributed to the absence of curiosity about the existence, meaning, and implications of the data of human wonder.

---

[1] Obviously, there are many other branches that could have been investigated, but it seemed best to limit myself to those branches that are most dominant and influential in the world today. I would also direct the reader to Appendix 1 that shows further research into The Dynamics of Knowing and Doing in various other languages of the world. Of course, a number of very large publications will need to be undertaken with which to achieve the ambitious goal of providing a massive presentation of the data of language universals in the many other languages that fall under the dominant branches as well as remaining branches of the linguistic tree. I wish to add, the data here may be absent of idiomatic subtlety that would be obvious to the expert and so I would humbly invite further correction and refinement by those who are fluent in the languages presented, either in this book, or in future publications of this linguistic data.

[2] Vicente Cantarino, *Modern Arabic Prose*. Indiana University Press, 1974, p. 135. [subsequently referred to as "Cantarino"]

[3] Dr. Syed Ali, *Arabic for Beginners*. New York: Hippocrene Books, 1994, is the source of this raw data.

[4] Vic Webb and Kembo-Sure, *African Voices*. Oxford University Press, 2000, p. 33.

[5] Wm. E. Welmers, *African Language Structures*. University of California Press, 1973, p. 7.

[6] Peter M. Wilson, *Simplified Swahili*. Nairobi: Longman Kenya Ltd., p. 77.

[7] *A Standard English-Swahili Dictionary*, Oxford University Press, 1953. This is the primary source of the data listed in this section unless otherwise specified.

[8] Alfons Loogman, *Swahili Grammar and Syntax*. Duquesne University Press, 1965, p. 235. [subsequently referred to as "Loogman"]
[9] Parker Po-fei Huang, *Cantonese Dictionary*. Yale University Press, 1970, p. xv. [subsequently referred to as "Huang"]
[10] Lars Ahrenberg, *Interrogative Structures of Swedish*. Uppsala University, 1987, p. 87. [subsequently referred to as "Ahrenberg"] Additional raw data, randomly classified by Ahrenberg, may be viewed in Appendix B.
[11] *Swedish-English Dictionary*, University of Minnesota Press, 1988. [All subsequent references are indicated by page number in parentheses.]
[12] The source of this research on German intonation is taken from http://coral.lili.uni-bielefeld.de/~gibbon/Hirst96/german96/node5.html. I have added italics for the purpose of emphasis. See the table in Appendix C. Additional random raw data, classified by Lederer, may be viewed in Appendix C.
[13] The expressions below are taken from C. Eckhard-Black, R. Whittle, *Cassell's Contemporary German*. New York: Simon and Schuster, 1992.

7

A DIALECTICAL ANALYSIS OF INVESTIGATION INTO LANGUAGE UNIVERSALS

In this chapter, we draw attention to a dominant culture of investigation of language universals that has systematically eclipsed curiosity about the existence, meaning, and implications of the data of human wonder – the core-attitudes we have formally identified as the grounding language universals. This culture, which is deeply rooted in present-day academic life, is clearly evident in the writing of a group of distinguished and very influential thinkers[1] who have sought to achieve progress in the search for language universals.[2] And so, in Chapter 7, we identify the symptoms of this culture, as well as their root causes, which permeate this writing.[3]

A book could be written (and needs to be written) about this pervasive culture. At its core is an ethos of self-neglect and truncation that has two root causes, a pernicious presence I would call the "Scylla and Charybdis" of inquiry into language universals.[4] We will come to that later, but first, we identify what is meant by self-neglect and truncation. "The neglected subject does not know himself. The truncated subject not only does not know himself but also is unaware of his ignorance and so, in one way or another, concludes that what he does not know does not exist."[5] Oddly enough, we receive some encouragement to free ourselves from this grip, from within the culture itself, in the Preface to *The Foundations of Language* by Ray Jackendoff:

> In order...to succeed, probably everyone will have to endure some discomfort and give a little....My own attitude is that we are in this together. It is going to take us lots of tools to understand language....We should try to appreciate exactly what each of the tools we have is good for, and to recognize when new and as yet undiscovered tools are necessary....[W]hat is called for is an open-mindedness to insights from whatever quarter...in the interests of deeper understanding. To my mind, that's what the game of science is about.[6]

And so, along with Jackendoff's sincere appeal, I encourage any language user, let alone those who identify language study with their professional task, to cultivate "an open-mindedness to insights" into the core-attitudes that we have empirically brought to light, the expression of which can be found in the two diagrams in Chapter 5. No doubt, the call for self-attention in the bold statements to follow will create some healthy "discomfort," but at the same time, we hope it will create an impetus toward advancing "the interests of deeper understanding" in a way that would lift the plausibility of Noam Chomsky's fantasy of a "new scientific civilization"[7] from an ideal that is "as yet undiscovered," to the accepted fact of human senseAbility.[8]

We begin with the obvious fact that the acquisition of language distinguishes the human from mere animality. What is not obvious to the ethos of self-neglect and truncation is that humans have an undefined senseAbility, driven by "the effective emergence of wonder, of the desire to understand."[9] Sadly, the ethos of self-neglect and truncation has resisted directing any serious curiosity toward our undefined senseAbility and its history. Thus, we focus initially on a claim that Pinker makes about cognitive science in his popular book, *The Language Instinct*, because it draws out the impact this ethos has had on discerning philosophy's role in formulating the science of cognition. "[S]ome thirty-five years ago a new science was born. Now called 'cognitive science,' it combines tools from psychology, computer science, linguistics, philosophy and neurobiology to explain the workings of human intelligence."[10] This perspective overlooks the fact that cognitive science was born in 4th Century B.C. when Aristotle, after years of laboring "to explain the workings of human intelligence," made his famous empirical observation about wonder being a beginning in the first sentence of the *Metaphysics*.[11] But this is not only Pinker's oversight. This oversight has dominated generation after generation of written reflection on the relationship between language and the workings of human intelligence.

We will be looking into the causes of why these efforts have bogged down – why writers have failed to undertake serious empirical inquiry into their core wonder, let alone take a luminous stand on its meaning and implications – a stand Aristotle and

Aquinas took when they paid attention to themselves in certain activities of curiosity. The potential to take a luminous stand has been replaced by an ethos of discouragement that has lead investigators to read Aristotle's famous first sentence about 'wonder being a beginning' as a mere piece of philosophical information. Consequently, we are drawing attention to an ethos of *how to read*. What Lonergan has to say about reading is extremely important. Here he happens to be speaking about Aquinas, but the message could be the same for Aristotle or any other serious person in history.

> Inasmuch as one may suppose that one already possesses a habitual understanding similar to that of Aquinas, no method or effort is needed to understand as Aquinas understood; one has simply to read, and the proper acts of understanding will follow. But one may not be ready to make that assumption on one's own behalf. Then one has to learn. Only by the slow, repetitious, circular labour of going over and over the data, by catching here a little insight and there another, by following through false leads and profiting from many mistakes, by continuous adjustments and cumulative changes of one's initial suppositions and perspectives and concepts can one hope to attain such a development of one's own understanding as to hope to understand what Aquinas understood and meant.[12]

By extension, we are also dealing with an ethos that espouses the illusion that the principle upon which Aristotle and Aquinas took their stand is just another "theory;" it is a destructive attitude that distorts the very meaning and role of theory itself.

> What, we may ask, does that word regularly mean? You have, perhaps, heard the statement 'that is just theory,' 'you're just theorizing.' The implication in such statements is that theory is unrelated to real situations, can even be trivial. This is a case of a word's original meaning being twisted by poor thinking.[13]

This attitude ignores the fact that "theoretical understanding...seeks to solve problems, to erect syntheses, to embrace the universe in a single view. Neither its existence, nor its value, nor the remote possibility of its success is denied. Still common sense is concerned not with remote but with proximate possibilities."[14] In his condemnation of this destructive attitude, Lonergan introduces the name "haute vulgarization" to describe it:

> Again, there can be acknowledged both theory and common sense but the acknowledgement of theory is a devalued acknowledgement. It is simply through what the French call 'haute vulgarization.' People have great respect for the great theoretical names – Newton and Einstein, Aristotle and Aquinas, weren't they wonderful people! – but they have no personal experience of the intellectual pattern of living, of what it is to live the way the theorist lives, to have that pure domination of the intellect as a part-time mode of one's subjectivity. They do not know by experience what that is, they are not familiar, strictly and accurately, with any field of theoretical objects. They have a very inadequate notion of what theory is....They are lost in some no man's land between the world of theory and the world of common sense.[15]

The ethos of vague commonsense "reading," along with its distortion of the meaning and role of "theory," generates a warped sort of writing that is "twisted by poor thinking." The self-attention required for scientific thinking to track properly is fixated out. "Thinking is something we all do, however badly, unless we have some neurochemical defects. Critical thinking can occur when we are luminous, clear, about what we are doing when we are thinking."[16] The achievement of critical thinking that would result from self-attention to the dynamics of wonder has been substituted by an ethos of "haute vulgarization" trapped in the commonsense eloquence of warped language.

This ethos is unabashedly reinforced, for example, in Jerry Fodor's famous thesis "that the central cognitive processes are not amenable to investigation; while the input systems have problem status, the central systems have mystery status; we can handle problems, but mysteries are beyond us."[17] Such precipitant pronouncements provoke some embarrassing questions:[18] for instance, on what precise basis does Fodor make a distinction between "problems" and "mysteries"? Furthermore, on what precise basis does he generate the terms, "central cognitive processes," "investigation," "input systems," "problem status," "central systems," "mystery status"? Sadly, it is telling how this vaguely speculative, pseudo-scientific use of language could pass muster as an expression of understanding in the massively complex field of cognition and language. For again we would note that after the initial mastery of language there emerges the capacity and need to elevate talk to the explanatory level, the achievement of which is the occurrence of direct insight into the what- and why-meaning lurking behind the expression. Yet Fodor's language is warped by a propensity to avoid that search. How can he *know* that the "central cognitional processes are not amenable to investigation" if he does not properly *understand* the object to which the name "central cognitional processes" refers? Luminous self-attention would have exposed this precipitance of failing to arrive where it should have begun, with a question mark, not a full stop. Moreover, his truncated expression veils the mistaken assumption that a nominal (verbal) insight is equivalent to an explanatory insight (understanding):

> What constitutes the difference? Both nominal and explanatory definitions suppose insights. But a nominal definition supposes no more than an insight into the proper use of language. An explanatory definition, on the other hand, supposes a further insight into the object to which language refers. The name, circle, is defined as a perfectly round plane curve, as the name, straight line, is defined as a line lying evenly between its extremes. But when one goes on to affirm that all radii in a circle are equal or that all right angles are equal, one no longer is talking merely of names. One is making assertions about the objects which names denote.[19]

We will be tackling the two root causes of this sort of warped language shortly.[20] First, we note that Herbert Butterfield attributes its currency to "extra-scientific" opinion that has gripped writers working in a literary tradition. Of this tradition he observes:

> ...it is important to note that the great movement of the eighteenth century was a literary one – it was not the new discoveries of science in that epoch but, rather, the French *philosophe* movement that decided the next turn in the story and determined the course Western civilization was to take....[The

> French writer] Fontenelle, as well as later writers of the *philosophe* movement, adopted the policy of making the intellectual work palatable and easy....[21]

The regrettable impact of that shift gave writers license to dodge scientific thinking, make "intellectual work palatable and easy," and attribute to common sense a status that is beyond its capability.[22]

> Whereas "reason" had once been a thing that required to be disciplined by a long and intensive training, the very meaning of the word began to change – now any man could say that he had it.... "Reason," in fact, came to signify much more what we today should call common sense.[23]

The disastrous consequences of extra-scientific opinion are reflected in J. L. Synge's comment concerning the psychology of mathematics:

> Such things may strike us as strange and rather fascinating, a strand of queerness enlivening the dull desert of scientific thought, arid stretches of logic. We may dismiss them lightly and pass on to the serious consideration of what thought and understanding are in terms of the words that philosophers have been accustomed to use. But we may be quite wrong in this. We may miss the turning leading to an understanding of understanding.[24]

Thus, the warped expression of extra-scientific opinion has colonized language in such a way as to exclude understanding from the process of how to read.[25] As Butterfield observes:

> It will concern us particularly to take note of those cases in which men not only solved a problem but had to alter their mentality in the process, or at least discovered afterwards that the solution involved a change in their mental approach."[26]

It is clear that writers in the culture of extra-scientific opinion, such as Fodor, have dismissed them "lightly," and have missed the "turning" that would naturally "alter their mentality in the process." And as we shall see, Fodor is not alone in this. Still, it must be asked: *why* is this so? It is time to tackle the two root causes: and so, with further examples from the field of language studies, I sketch the character of, first, conceptualism,[27] and secondly, its offspring, commonsense eclecticism.[28]

Conceptualism[29] has its origin in Duns Scotus' view of mind:[30]

> The Scotist rejection of insight into phantasm necessarily reduced the act of understanding to seeing a nexus between concepts; hence, while for Aquinas understanding precedes conceptualization, which is rational, for Scotus understanding is preceded by conceptualization…[31]

And so, Scotus' positing of concepts first, eclipses the act of direct understanding. To illustrate, the polarity between the act of direct understanding and conceptualism may be summarized by two options for how to read the two diagrams in Chapter 5.[32] Let the first option, representing direct understanding, be called MAC where 'M' refers to Mind (our mind) 'A' has the meaning of Ah? (What?) and Aha! (direct insight) and 'C' refers to concept, formulation, definition. So we have M?!C as representing the lower part of the diagram: our Mind homes in on (?) some experience, to reach (perhaps with a great deal of struggle) an insight (!), which makes it possible for us to generate a concept, to beget a definition.[33] Note there is a gap that can be too easily dodged. How do we get from ? to !. Why is this gap so easily dodged? That's because of the other view, represented by conceptualism, which we now call McA. Here again we mean *mind* by 'M' and *concept* by 'C.' What is meant by 'A'? Instead of ? and ! here, 'A' means Analysis. What is this other view saying to us? That we have a mind; that 'somehow' we can get concepts; that these concepts need analysis so we can become clear on their content. The assumption of the conceptualist position is that reading, repeating, memorizing, looking at, or describing an idea is the same as understanding it. The two views are in clear opposition: either insight comes before concept (MAC), or it comes from analysis afterwards (McA).[34]

And so, once again, I invite you, the reader, the language user, the language study professional, to appreciate, in a most elementary way, what Lonergan meant by "the monster that has stood forth in our day."[35] The task of exorcising the beast begins by finding a credible way either to agree or to disagree in principle with what Aristotle claims is a beginning,[36] with what Aquinas claims "[w]e can all experience in ourselves."[37] Again, ask yourself, am I a specimen of what Aristotle and Aquinas are talking about? And does asking yourself this question, in your own words, provide you with an empirically sound principle upon which to take a concrete stand about your undefined senseAbility, in the spontaneity of your *Questions and Answers*?[38]

A few self-attentive empirical stabs at this exercise in how to read the diagrams would yield enough personal data with which to determine the view that represents our core wonder. But in the examples of truncated thinking and writing presented below the assumption is, concept comes first; consequently, self-attentive empirical stabs at the activity on wonder is, so to speak, "bracketed out." The method applied to the problem of language, in each case, parallels the conceptualist, extra-scientific approach we observed of Fodor.

First, for Noam Chomsky, "The same question arises, as a question of science[39]…Thus language is a mirror of mind in a deep and significant sense. It is a product of human intelligence, created anew in each individual by operations that lie far beyond the reach of will or consciousness[40] [and] "where we deal with cognitive structures, either in a mature state of knowledge and belief or in the initial state, we face problems[41]…When we ask how humans make use of these cognitive structures, how and why they make choices and behave as they do, although there is much that we can say as human beings with intuition and insight, there is little that we can say as scientists."[42] Chomsky's language, far from grounded by an appreciation of his own inner dynamic reality, is warped by a conceptualist use of the terms 'mind,' 'intelligence,' 'will,' 'consciousness,' 'cognitive structures,' 'knowledge,' 'belief,' and 'science'. Again, his reference to "operations that lie far beyond the reach of will or consciousness," exercises judgment without the prior act of understanding. Lurking within this assumption are unanswered what-questions with respect to "operations," "will," and "consciousness." Moreover, he claims to speak profoundly of 'intuition' and 'insight' while, at the same time, asserts that there is little one can say as a scientist. Lurking within this assumption are unanswered what-questions with respect to "intuition," and "insight." Paradoxically, his use of the adverbs 'how,' and 'why,' rather than explaining, explain away. The act of direct understanding is negated; these expressions of quest are held hostage by conceptualist language; neither the data of language, nor the data of quest come under serious empirical or theoretical scrutiny.

Secondly, in the fourth chapter of *The Language Instinct*, titled "How Language Works," Steven Pinker warps the language of quest in the paragraph below.

> This is the essence of the language instinct: language conveys news. The streams of words called 'sentences' are not just memory prods...they tell you who in fact did what to whom...Language allows us to know how octopuses make love and how to remove cherry stains and why Tad was heartbroken, and whether the Red Sox will win the World Series without a good relief pitcher and how to build an atom bomb in your basement and how Catherine the Great died, among other things.[43]

Pinker marginalizes the function of the adverbs 'how' and 'why.' One way in which this is manifest is by his brushing aside the human search for "essence." He does not seriously follow-up on the core what- and why-attitude that calls for the possession of rule, form, essence, definition. Moreover, he shows the common tendency of conceptualism to equate informing with understanding. By marginalizing these powerful expressions of quest, Pinker abandons the sign "?" that marks the search, renders these powerful words inert, and trivializes the topic by assuming he can inform the audience of his "idea." When Pinker writes: "I think that our understanding of language offers a more satisfying way of studying the human mind and human nature,"[44] what precisely does he mean by "I think," "understanding," "mind," and "human nature"? What does he mean when he refers to "words," "fact," "what"? Such impoverished language of conceptualism lacks the required "observation [that] distinguishes moments in the genesis of a definition....The pivot between images and concepts is the insight. And setting the standard which insight, images, and concepts must meet is the question...."[45] In other words, "Definitions do not occur in a private vacuum of their own. They emerge in solidarity with experiences, images, questions and insights."[46]

Thirdly, the more technical writing of Bernard Comrie in *Language Universals and Linguistic Typology*, is troubled throughout by lack of serious self-discovery. His statement, "it is necessary for us to make some preliminary remarks on the nature of definition,"[47] is never followed up by a luminous analysis of his own core wonder. Again, his discussion of the "universal aspects of the grammatical subject"[48] does not properly focus on an explanatory heuristics of "the notion of a thing" and its usages.[49] His considerations of "universal tendencies in the syntax and semantics of causative constructions"[50] fail to move beyond a vague human view of efficient causality to a methodological precision regarding five causal categories and differentiations of question structures.[51] In the first chapter, Comrie discusses perspectives on the search for universals of language. "[T]he best way to learn about language universals is by the detailed study of a small number of languages; such linguists have also advocated stating language universals in terms of abstract structures and have tended to favour innateness as the explanation for language universals."[52] Innateness, of course, brings Chomsky to mind, and the popularity it enjoys. Comrie points out the problems associated with various versions of 'innatism,' and he concludes, regarding learning a first language, that

> it cannot be the case that the language as a whole is innate – note that this was established on the basis of empirical observation, rather than by speculation. At best certain principles common to all human languages would be innate, which would thus facilitate the child's task in acquiring whichever language he happens to be exposed to, with no preference for one language over any other. This now brings in the last link in this argument: since the abstract principles claimed to be innate are the same for all children, irrespective of

ethnic background, they must be neutral with respect to differences among languages, i.e. they must be universal.[53]

Comrie's conjecture that "certain principles common to all human languages would be innate" negates his favouring of empirical observation.[54] His vague use of the term "principle" lacks the heuristic control of self-discovery; his meaning is more like that of an axiom.[55] Moreover, his vague use of the term "abstract," which he oddly juxtaposes to the term "principle," is also caught in this truncated snare.[56] It misrepresents the use of this term and its role in theory: "To abstract is not 'to leave out' or 'to take out' but to 'add on'."[57] Instead of following through properly with an empirical what- and why-search, he trivializes its function to a simple reduction of meaning.[58]

Fourthly, Jacques Derrida, while acknowledging the deficiency of vague description, is also trapped by truncated language. He writes, "indeed, one must understand this incompetence of science which is also the incompetence of philosophy, the closure of the epistémè[59]...it is a question of...access to another system linking speech and writing[60] ...Whatever it might be, the movement of the retreat of the signifier, the perfecting of writing, would free attention and consciousness (knowledge and self-knowledge as idealization of the mastered object) for the presence of the signified."[61] Derrida's language is prodigious in its manipulation of scientific terminology, but its use is not enriched by self-attention. Sadly, Derrida truncates the very scientific language he would seek to elevate. First, he shifts the language of wonder from a question to a statement, "it is a question of," and secondly, his meaning of words like 'understand,' 'science,' 'is,' 'question,' 'consciousness,' 'knowledge,' 'self-knowledge,' 'object,' and so on, is short circuited by his failure to 'free attention' to the data of his own curiosity.

And so, in acknowledging that "understanding can be mimicked by an air of profundity, a glow of self-importance, a power to command respectful attention, because the attainment of insight is a hidden event and its content a secret that does not admit communication,"[62] Lonergan laments, "to many profound minds, so brief a description seems to have been insufficient.

Scotus flatly denied the fact of insight into phantasm. Kant['s]...critique was not of the pure reason but of the human mind as conceived by Scotus....Though the point is elementary, still it is so important that I beg to be permitted to dwell on a plain matter of fact."[63] The fact about truncated language is, the activities represented by the symbols ? and ! in which analysis occurs *prior to* the formulation of concept (MAC), are missing, and have been replaced by the symbol 'A' in which the activity of 'analysis' occurs *after* the concept has been named (McA).

An offshoot of that neglect is the habitual tendency to make statements out of questions, to "dismiss [questions] lightly and pass on to the serious consideration of what thought and understanding are in terms of the words that philosophers have been accustomed to use."[64] And so this ethos of conceptualist writing may raise the questions, but because their role has been reduced to that of literary rhetorical devices, the questions are never followed up on properly. Instead, truncated language usage is satisfied to describe what thought and understanding is like. But what *do* these writers mean by the name "insight"? What does "ask himself" mean? What is meant by "struck a note in his imagination"? What is the activity of "pushing this idea"? Above all, what is meant by the sign "?," which is generously placed throughout all kinds of writing about the search for language universals. This sign cannot be named "it," because "it" cannot be called a letter or an ideogram, since it marks, without a neat name, a search, not an idea. And as we have seen, naming "it" can only occur after having posed the question that marks the beginning of self-attention: "What am I doing when I puzzle like this?" *These* questions are not rhetorical.

The truncated treatment of questions dominates what are called wh-Conferences in linguistic studies. The focus of attention is not on the questing subjects that are present at such events. These scholars may claim, "of course not: the focus is on field work, samples, whatever." But if one does not understand one's own "wh-ing," what is one making of the sample's "wh-ing?" And so a further example of neglect of one's own "wh-ing" occurs in John A. Hawkes' *Explaining Language Universals*,[65] the title of which precisely identifies our topic. But our searching pivots on asking, literally, What's "what" in focusing on questions, yet the book's sole entry under "Q" is "quantifier scope." The first paragraph of the book, laced with question marks, resonates with the language of quest: "Why do languages share the universal principals that they do? Why do they exhibit the parameters that they do? The purpose of this volume is to address such questions and to provide new insights, clarifications, critical discussion, new data." Yet the book passes over its own question marks – a metaphor for the author's self-neglect – and misses data essential to this bubbling field.[66]

Conceptualism operates in tandem with its offspring: common-sense eclecticism.[67] For Lonergan, "while common-sense eclecticism discourages the effort to understand, it encourages a wide exercise of judgment. But this is to overlook the fact that understanding is a constitutive component in knowledge, that before one can pass judgment on any issue, one has to understand it."[68] Because the judgments of Hawkes, Fodor, Jackendoff, Comrie, Derrida, Chomsky and Pinker are devoid of what Lonergan calls "prolonged efforts at introspective analysis, [they] could not say just what occurs in the reflective insight, [therefore] to pronounce judgment without that reflective understanding is merely to guess...."[69] It is disturbing to contemplate that the ethos of extra-scientific opinion that dominates academic life actually rests on a patchwork of "guesses." It systematically[70] looks to common-sense eclecticism for its method. For Lonergan, "The fallacy of this procedure is, of course, that it fails to grasp the limitations of common sense...it is vain to ask common sense to provide the philosophic concepts, to formulate the coherent range of possible positions, to set the questions that can be answered by an appeal to commonly known facts..."[71] We find this sort of tendency in a passage from Jackendoff:

> ...the conceptualist approach shifts the focus of semantics from the question 'What makes sentences true?' to what I take to be the more ecologically sound question, 'How do we humans understand language...How can anyone rely on someone else's report of an observation, and how can anyone count on others' usage of language? Turned a different way: if conceptualization is essentially personal, how can we communicate... This is now

getting quite speculative, but I am inclined to think that human beings have a need to 'tune' their conceptualizations to those of others – to have a common understanding of the world. Since we cannot read minds, the only way we can assess our attunement is by judging whether the behavior of others – including what they say – makes sense. To the extent that all members of a community are effective in acting on this drive, there will be a tendency for conceptual convergence, including in the use of language.[72]

His urge to "'tune' their conceptualizations to those of others...to assess our attunement... by judging whether the behavior of others...makes sense," reflects an aimlessness that, "while discouraging understanding, urges one to paw through the display of opinions..."[73]

We conclude the chapter on a note of pessimism for language studies as it pertains to the present. The collective babble and Babel of self-neglect and truncation will continue its systematic eclipse of curiosity about the existence, meaning, and implications of the data of human wonder – the core-attitudes we have formally identified the grounding language universals "because their efforts are prior to the discovery of those criteria, because their pure desire to know is not contrasted with all their other desires, because names and heuristic anticipations can be mistaken for insights..."[74] A clear understanding of procedure and method in fact pivots on a fundamental insight into one's activity of knowing and doing. Such insights might arise if the community of thinkers writing in language studies seriously committed themselves to directing their attention to questing senseAbility and their own data of quest. Our next step, in Chapter 8, heralds a more optimistic future by introducing the essential features of the two principles necessary for successful restructuring in language studies, and by working out the challenge of meeting its implications. And so we do but turn yet another page in our adventure.

---

[1] The examples will be taken from the writing of Noam Chomsky, Steven Pinker, Jerry Fodor, Bernard Comrie, Jacques Derrida, John A. Hawkes and Ray Jackendoff.

² I cannot resist adding this personal anecdote regarding the need for progress in language study. It is the true story of a learned professor (whose name and institution will remain anonymous) who saw no merit or value in the goal of this project. His advice to me was to accept that progress was "orthogonal" to the study of linguistics and that abandoning progress as a goal would be a step toward making progress.

³ This task of dialectic analysis covers a very broad range of human knowledge. I restrict my investigation to those causes that have had the most proximate impact in the field of language studies. For a full account, see Lonergan, "The Dialectic of Method in Metaphysics," op. cit., *Insight*, pp. 401-430 [426-55].

⁴ References to this ethos abound in the writing of McShane and Lonergan. In capturing the mood of this fundamental disorientation of modern inquiry, Lonergan borrows the term "haute vulgarization" from the French language in Bernard Lonergan, *Philosophical and Theological Papers 1958-1964 (CWL 6)*, University of Toronto Press, 1966, p. 121. [subsequently referred to as *Philosophical and Theological Papers*]

⁵ Op. cit., *The Subject*, p. 8.

⁶ Ray Jackendoff, *Foundations of Language*. Oxford University Press, 2002, p. xiii.

⁷ I refer to Chomsky's view of "a new scientific civilization in which 'animal nature' is transcended and human nature can truly flourish." Noam Chomsky, *Reflections on Language*. New York: Pantheon Books, 1975, p. 134.

⁸ Perhaps it is useful to think of these diagrams as a sort of parallel to the diagram of the periodic table, found in the beginning of chemistry textbooks. The periodic table took centuries to discover and it now points students and researchers towards areas in need of detailed investigation if we are to make progress in chemistry. The diagrams to which we refer took centuries to discover and, furthermore, they are not yet generally accepted the way the periodic table is generally accepted.

⁹ Op. cit., *Insight*, p. 10 [34].

¹⁰ Steven Pinker, *The Language Instinct*. New York: William Morrow & Co., 1994, p. 17. Please note, I am not dismissing the legitimacy of these disciplines and their relevance to language; I am, however, pointing out the serious impact that the tradition of dodging scientific thinking has had on them.

¹¹ A simple illustration of dodging scientific thinking about "cognition" can be accomplished by engaging in an exercise of looking in the index of textbooks in these subject-areas under the letter "Q" for references to "question" "or question-structures." They are rarely, if ever, found. On the odd occasion they do turn up, the writer's focus is not adequately empirical, but vaguely conjectural. I would add that no indexed reference is made to "question" in *The Language Instinct*. Richard McKeon's "General Introduction" to Aristotle further reinforces Pinker's restricted historical perspective on "science." See, "Scientific Method in the Philosophy of Aristotle." McKeon writes, "Aristotle's philosophy consists in his contributions to the sciences and his reflections on the interrelations among the sciences, for even metaphysics, which he called 'first philosophy,' was one of the theoretic sciences, and its

subject matter included the study of the principles of the other sciences. The interest in the structure and system of the sciences leads Aristotle into frequent inquiries into the origins of the sciences, both in the historical sense of tracing the development of particular doctrines or the course of investigation of particular problems and in the formal sense of setting forth the requirements of scientific inquiry and proof...Aristotle was convinced that he had himself originated most of what was sound and precise...in his own inquiry on method..." Op. cit., *Introduction to Aristotle*, pp. xiii-xiv.

[12] Op. cit., *Verbum*, p. 223.
[13] Op. cit., *ICT*, p. 148.
[14] Op. cit., *Insight*, p. 417 [442].
[15] Op. cit., *Philosophical and Theological Papers*, p. 121.
[16] The clear distinction between poor thinking and proper thinking is discussed in Chapter 8 when we introduce Generalized Empirical Method, the basis for critical thinking. Op. cit., *ICT*, p. 142.
[17] *Linguistics: The Cambridge Survey*, Vol. III. Cambridge University Press, 1988, (ed.) F.J. Newmeyer, p. 57.
[18] Flawed pronouncements such as Foder's can easily be given the status of fact and so dominate a field lacking "an appropriate language...There follows an inflation, or devaluation, of this language and so of the doctrine it conveys....Doctrines that are embarrassing will not be mentioned in polite company." (*Method*, p. 299)
[19] Op. cit., *Insight*, p. 11 [35].
[20] This point anticipates the topic that runs through Chapters 8 to 10. For an introduction to the historical perspective, I would suggest as a beginning, *BHT*, pp. 37-41.
[21] Herbert Butterfield, *The Origin of Modern Science*. Toronto: Clarke, Irwin & Co., 1968, pp. 166-70.
[22] In Chapter 8 we provide an example of how extra-scientific attitudes can extend even to scientists working in the field of physics.
[23] Ibid., pp. 166-70.
[24] J.L. Synge, *Science, Sense and Nonsense*. London: Cape, 1951, p. 112.
[25] I borrow the expression of colonization from Declan Kibberd, *Inventing Irleland. The Literature of the Modern Nation*. Harvard University Press, 1993. The index under *colonization* gives abundant references to the problems of colonized expression. To the issue of the redemptive character of such literatures as the Anglo-Irish, Anglo-Indian and Anglo-African there must be added the deeper problem of the disorientation. A simple instance of false orientation, a colonization of Scotus' view of mind in almost all brands of educated English, is the recurrence of phrases like "understanding the concept of," "teaching the concept of," "clarifying the concept of." Such orientations murder the educational process: neither child nor adult mind fits this linguistic mold.
[26] Ibid., p. viii.
[27] It is also important to note, in this matter of dead language, that I offer a mere verbal description here (or more precisely, raw data masquerading as

familiar names) and would warn the reader that the danger of conceptualism is an ever-present reality, the result of contemporary educational schemes of *how to read*. For instance, one might well be under the illusion that understanding occurs merely by reading the typed words on the page, assuming that the meaning is obviously 'there to be seen,' to be agreed or disagreed with. There is the further fallacy of denying meaning simply because it does not show up as black marks on a page!

[28] Op. cit., *Insight*, p. 416 [441]. See Section 4.4, "Common-Sense Eclecticism," pp. 416-21 [441-46].

[29] "As insights fulfill three functions, so conceptualism has three basic defects." See op. cit., *The Subject*, pp. 9-12.

[30] This basic issue is described in op. cit., *Verbum*, pp. 38-9. See Chapter One, Part 4, "Insight into Phantasm," *Verbum*, pp. 38-46.

[31] Op. cit., *Verbum*, p. 39.

[32] Op. cit., *ICT*, p. 65.

[33] Needless to say, this summary has to be backed up by illustrations, by puzzles, etc. and messed with in private.

[34] Op. cit., *ICT*, pp. 64-66. Conceptualism came to be called 'conceptual analysis,' which was a name for a British tradition of philosophy in the last century.

[35] Op. cit., *Method*, p. 40. The challenge of taking this stand is brutally expressed by Lonergan: "What I want to communicate on this talk about art is the notion that art is relevant to concrete living, that it is an exploration of the potentialities of concrete living. That exploration is extremely important in our age, when philosophers for at least two centuries, through doctrines on politics, economics, education, and through ever further doctrines, have been trying to remake man, and have done not a little to make life unlivable." *Method*, p. 232. For further encouragement and perspective, see Philip McShane: "How does one read sentences like "the social situation deteriorates cumulatively," (*Insight*, 229[254]) "the culture has become a slum," (*Method*, p. 99) "such is the monster that has stood forth in our day" (*Method*, p. 40)? Over previous decades I have emphasized to audiences that great ugliness is as remote as great beauty: the monster calls for a massive dedication of aesthetic detecting. I recall now my own first reading, in the winter of 1957-8, of Aquinas' reflection on happiness. I had already begun my reading of that central section of *Insight* on the sell-out of global culture: fifty years later I begin to sense the Shostakovitch symphony of that cording. But as I read Aquinas then it dawned on me - how naively truncated can you be? - that this chap meant what he said. "Does human happiness consist in ....?"; "I say, No." [This is his common manner of beginning his response, except that his questions are so put that he can say, I reply: Yes". Aristotle, too, is speaking for and about himself as he moves through the *Nicomachean Ethics* towards his view on the lonely excellence of contemplation. One would benefit by reading these two chaps together, see how they weave forward.] Fifty years later I can detect, with some level of luminosity, the place of Aquinas within the

challenge of taking a stand, in later cycles of incline. [The full dialectic procedure of *Method* page 250 relocates, discomfortingly, the meeting with Aristotle and Aquinas.] *www.philipmcshane.ca*, Prehumous, "Teaching Highschool Economics. A Common-Quest Manifesto," p. 42.

[36] Op. cit., *Metaphysics*. Book A (I).
[37] St. Thomas Aquinas. *Summa Theologiae*. 1, q. 84, a. 7 c.
[38] The title of a book, *Questions and Answers*, F. Keifer (ed.) Dordrecht: D. Reidel, 1983, an encouraging topic with a disappointing perspective in which reflection on question and answers is written in language that is estranged from human 'senseAbility.' As we shall see in the examples to follow, the use/abuse of language that is all too common in today's academic environment that 'flattens' statements about questions, brushes aside questions about questions, with a common tendency to 'talk around' their questions. In one of the articles with the promising title reflecting our present interest, "New foundations for a theory of questions and answers," curiosity with respect to his own questions is entirely absent in Jaakko Hintikka's truncated description: "[i]t is in effect a conceptualization of knowledge as an objective informational notion" (p. 159).
[39] Op. cit., *Reflections on Language*, p. 5.
[40] Ibid., p. 4.
[41] See Op. cit., *Insight*, p. 417 [442]: "Theoretical understanding, then, seeks to solve problems, to erect syntheses, to embrace the universe in a single view. Neither its existence, nor its value, nor the remote possibility of its success is denied."
[42] Op. cit., *Reflections on Language*, pp. 138-9.
[43] Op. cit., *The Language Instinct*, p. 83.
[44] Ibid., *The Language Instinct*, p. 407.
[45] Op. cit., *Insight*, p. 10 [35].
[46] Ibid., p. 11 [36]. "Linguistics remains comfortably truncated, nor does it take vast self-attention to glimpse, e.g., the sorry truncation of Steven Pinker's lauded summation of things linguistic, *The Language Instinct*, Penguin, 1995. (E.g. his "Big Bang" discussion just does not cut it, ontogenetically or phylogenetically)." Philip McShane, *The Redress of Poise: The End of Lonergan's Work*, www.philipmcshane.ca, p. xii.
[47] Ibid., p. 106.
[48] Ibid., pp. 104-125.
[49] See op. cit., *Insight*, Chapter VIII, "Things."
[50] Ibid., p. 175.
[51] Op. cit., *Redress of Poise*, p. xii. See Chapter 3.
[52] Op. cit., *Language Universals and Linguistic Typology*, p. 29.
[53] Ibid., pp. 3-4.
[54] Ibid., p. 5.
[55] See op. cit., *Verbum*, pp. 68-9.
[56] The term 'abstract' is a large issue with respect to language crippled by conceptualism. See op. cit., *The Subject*, pp. 9-12. "A defect of conceptualism is

an excessive abstractness. For the generalities of our knowledge are related to concrete reality in two distinct manners. There is the relation of the universal to the particular, of man to *this* man, of circle to *this* circle. There is also the far more important relation of the intelligible to the sensible, of the unity or pattern grasped by insight to the data in which the unity or pattern is grasped. Now this second relation, which parallels the relation of form to matter, is far more intimate than the first. The universal abstracts from the particular, but the intelligibility, grasped by insight, is imminent in the sensible and, when the sensible datum, image, symbol, is removed, the insight vanishes. But conceptualism ignores human understanding and so it overlooks the concrete mode of understanding that grasps intelligibility in the sensible itself. It is confined to a world of abstract universals, and its only link with the concrete is the relation of universal to particular."

[57] Op. cit., *BHT*, p. 68.

[58] There is the problem of general bias, a sort of global *flattening of meaning*. History has multiplied words, externalized them. The large issue of "The Dialectic of Community," and the perversion of "world process" come to mind. For enlargement on "General Bias," see op. cit., *Insight*, pp. 225-241 [250-69].

[59] Jacques Derrida, *Of Grammatology*. Spivak, G.C. (trans.) Johns Hopkins University Press, 1998, p. 93.

[60] Ibid., 93.

[61] Ibid., 287.

[62] Op. cit., *Insight*, p. 542 [566].

[63] Op. cit., *Verbum*, pp. 38-39.

[64] Op. cit., *Science, Sense and Nonsense*, p. 112.

[65] John A. Hawkes, *Explaining Language Universals*. Blackwells, Oxford, 1988.

[66] Op. cit., *BHT*, pp. 12-13.

[67] Op. cit., *Insight*, p. 416 [441]. See Section 4.4, "Common-Sense Eclecticism," pp. 416-21 [441-46].

[68] Ibid., p. 419 [444].

[69] Ibid., p. 279 [304].

[70] The large issue of "The Dialectic of Community," and the perversion of "world process" also surface here. See *Insight*, on the topic of "Individual," "Group," and "General Bias," pp. 225-244 [250-69]. The issue as it is related to the systematic component is raised in *Insight*, pp. 118-128 [141-51]. See "Emergent Probability" and "Schemes of Recurrence."

[71] Op. cit., *Insight*, p. 419 [444].

[72] Op. cit., *Foundations of Language*, pp. 329-330.

[73] Ibid., p. 419 [444]. Aquinas' comment remains terribly true: inform students of a bundle of opinions and they depart empty-headedly. "*Nihil scientiae vel intellectus acquiret, sed vacuus adscedet*" (Quodl., IV, a. 18).

[74] Op. cit., *Insight*, p. 542 [566].

8

METHODOLOGICAL RE-STRUCTURING

Chapter 8 introduces the essential features of the two principles necessary for successful restructuring in language studies: first, a focal shift in grammatology and secondly, a functional relating of sub-fields of language. Originally, the principles emerged more clearly in the field of theology. In *Method in Theology*, Lonergan calls for a "framework for collaborative creativity."[1] In language studies, such a framework would "outline the various clusters of operations to be performed" by language scholars "when they go about their various tasks."[2]

In groping toward a solution in language studies, Jackendoff observed, "the only way...is by judging [what] makes sense. To the extent that all members of a community are effective in acting on this drive, there will be a tendency for conceptual convergence...."[3] Paul De Man initiates a move beyond Jackendoff's truncated description, toward a more precise strategy for a solution to the "main methodological difficulties that plague literary studies."[4] De Man's strategy anticipates the basis of both a focal shift in grammatology and a functional relating of sub-fields of language:

> From the start, we have at least four possible and distinct types of self: the self that judges, the self that reads, the self that writes, and the self that reads itself. The question of finding the common level on which these selves meet and thus of establishing the unity of a literary consciousness stands at the beginning of the main methodological difficulties that plague literary studies.[5]

By identifying "distinct types of self" De Man anticipates the principle behind our focal shift in grammatology. He foreshadows the strategy required with which to make this shift possible by drawing attention to "the self that reads itself," the process of which would necessitate a precise self-attention, the achievement of which has been shown to bring the zone of core grammar to light. By furnishing "the common level on which these selves meet and thus of establishing the unity of a literary consciousness," there is the seed of what De Man anticipates to be a principle behind a relating of sub-fields of language. So, the focus of De Man's search "stands at the beginning of the main methodological" shift to the two fundamental principles of language studies, the process of which Lonergan calls *Generalized Empirical Method* and *Functional Specialization*.[6]

Thus, we apply these principles to the broad field of language studies in this chapter and the next. We introduce the first principle, Generalized Empirical Method, as the fundamental ground for the restructuring. Then we relate it to the second principle, the eight-fold collaborative framework called Functional Specialization. The first principle is the basis of the focal shift in grammatology that we have gradually worked toward in the early chapters.[7] The second principle, Lonergan's crowning achievement, is a functional relating of subfields of language through a division of labour consisting of eight distinct but functionally related tasks that yield cumulative and progressive results.

1. Generalized Empirical Method[8]

Generalized Empirical Method (GEM) is the procedure of critical thinking that occurs when we are luminous, clear, about what we are doing when we are thinking. As such, it seeks to be luminous, clear, on the distinction between the horizon of common sense and the horizon of science. Furthermore, it seeks to be luminous, clear, on the polymorphism of human consciousness.[9] Thus, it is a method of living and learning and teaching that involves the proper mix of attention to human desire in its reach for everything and everyone and, at the same time, to what human desire is teaching. In Lonergan's terms,

> It does not treat of objects without taking into account the corresponding operations of the subject: it does not treat of the subject's operations without taking into account the corresponding objects.[10]

So, for example, if a language student, teacher or professional is studying any species of linguistic or literary data, that person is also self-studying the language student, teacher or professional. All are finding out about both the linguistic or literary data and the data of the student-teacher-professional. The task, then, is dually focused – to attend to oneself as linguistic or literary by asking: *"How am I studying linguistic or literary data?" "What am I doing when I am studying linguistic or literary data?"* GEM works because it lifts language studies out of the ethos of self-neglect and truncation, the domination of which we observed in Chapter 7, and replaces it with an empirical attitude that rises above vague metaphor in the search for an explanatory perspective.

For an illustration of the beginning of this lift we return to Aristotle. Recall that single sentence with which he begins his *Metaphysics*. Here we repeat that strategy by selecting a sentence from his *Poetics*.[11] So a single-sentence focus is an exercise against the general ethos in language studies such as the fallacy of easy reading, the fallacy of extra-scientific opinion, the fallacy of popularization,[12] fallacies about psychology, neuroscience,[13] or any other discipline tied to language studies.[14] Finally, the exercise puts the entire book in a quite new context of a future metascientific precision, enabling us to tackle it on a quite new level of meaning. What possible one-sentence topic in the *Poetics* could cause this transformation? It returns us to a childhood experience, an insight we all had, which needs understanding if we are to lift human studies out of truncated descriptiveness.

So, on to our single sentence: not a sweep through a form of art, but an apparently simple point regarding saying words like *eh, be, see, dee...el, em, en....* Words?? Let's hear, read, Aristotle talking about letters, letter-noises.

> Indivisible sounds are uttered by the brutes also, but no one of these is a letter in our sense of the term.[15]

"In our **sense** of the term?" What **is** my sense of the term, *letter*? What do I **mean** by *em*? The procedure, then, when dually focused, asks: "How am I studying the data referred to as "letter"?" "What am I doing when I am studying data referred to as "word"? We are reaching for a new focus expressed in these questions. What focus? Precisely. We are what-poised to move from the state of babbling to talk beyond the horizon of common sense. Appreciating that what-poise in ourselves could mean months or years of experimental science in savouring self-taste. Observe that our focus is precisely the "I" behind our eyes, the "I" in the questions, the "I" generating the insights both into the data and into our own senseAbility, toward being self-lifting, toward being a luminous self-presence. Noticing this self-presence is to notice our molecules, our neurochemistry, our reverberating physical, chemical, botanical, zoological, psychological, wonderful energy shifting in rhythmical patterns towards a luminous appreciation of ourselves as language users.[16] And so we are thrust into the exigencies of a scientific attitude in dual-process: a "turn to the idea" and a turn to the operations of the subject. It is a startling beginning to notice the complexity that involves following through properly on our what-questions, our spontaneous "whatting" drive to make "sense" in the patterns of marks and remarks.[17] It is a radical shift with the psychic resonance of a Wordsworthian intimation that "The earth, and every common sight, / To me did seem / Apparelled in celestial light, / The glory and the freshness of a dream."[18] And yet the task is to rise above metaphor and find the startling facts about the data that is assigned the name "letter" and "word," and, in the process, the data that is assigned the name "language user."[19] "At such a time, our academic reach for the adequate zoneview of organism or the melodies of tongue-organ must thus break beyond the disorientations of description."[20] In the meantime, "To say it all with the greatest brevity: one has not only to read [creative and reflective data in language studies] but also to discover oneself in oneself."[21] Brevity also prevents further detail here because

> this stuff is not introductory... Rather, it aims at 'opening up' the topic – and the reader discomfortingly. The discomfort relates to the fact that the pointers are uncompromisingly heuristic and explanatory. It is tough reading but, I suggest, worth attempting. It may help your discernment to move towards a sigh of relief – 'the thin air of theory is not for me' –

or towards a gallant bracing of your psyche – 'this is worth a life.'[22]

In this context, another illustration into the problem of word meanings was given, you will recall, by our venture into the moment of language in Helen Keller and in ourselves. We shared the question that surged through seven-year-old Helen Keller's bloodstream, the fact that all normal children in our times acquire language, that animals are somehow different. What makes the difference? Our venture there dramatically illustrates the beginning of how self-understanding would transform language studies. It is interesting to quote Lonergan's expression of the same challenge. It is brief and inadequate to present audiences. Do you agree? Or in reading this paragraph of Lonergan's, would you really have thought of pausing for an hour or a month or more to get to grips with this particular insight of language that you had when you were tiny? Here, Hear, then, the passage:

> The moment of language in human development is most strikingly illustrated by the story of Helen Keller's discovery that the successive touches made on her hand by her teacher conveyed names of objects. The moment when she first caught on was marked by the expression of profound emotion and, in turn, the emotion bore fruit in so powerful an interest that she signified her desire to learn and did learn the name of about twenty objects in a very short time. It was the beginning of an incredible career of learning.[23]

I would suggest, as a follow up to this pointing, and a worthwhile exercise for the adventurous, going back (or forward) to a fresh reading of Chapter 4, a sort of beginner's reshuffling of a language user's luminous self-appreciation. Again, one might return to earlier chapters and have a crack at the beginning of a luminous reaching for a new level of focus on one letter of one word in the many languages we have encountered that opens our I's to the data-for-us, to the data as exhibited to our senses.

Thus, we conclude our introduction to GEM. We took a single sentence from Aristotle's *Poetics* as a suggested start to a prolonged reflection on GEM. We have given pointers to the problem of Aristotle's claim and the challenge of leaving behind the truncated dodges of Chapter 7. The foregoing introductory description of how GEM proceeds, as well as the elementary illustration of its function and relevance, underscores the magnitude of the challenge to language studies in a manner that is both clear and direct – for the modest beginner in the present, GEM is a tough slow exercise that, if successful, would transform her/his reading of this or any other book. In the academic norm of the future, the success of GEM will facilitate self-luminosity with which to "transform the axial barbarian. 'Such is the monster that has stood forth in our day.'"[24]

2. Functional Specialization[25]

> Gather
> No moss you rolling stones
> Nothing thought out atones
> For no flight
> In the light.[26]

Lonergan's lasting achievement, Functional Specialization, represents a fresh start for methodology in language studies. We will primarily focus on its structure below. We begin with the same basic question as in the previous section on GEM: what is a word, what is language? Yet it is to be tackled now not by turning to ourselves but by turning towards the results of language studies. This is not too peculiar a direction: What is language? It is what is studied in linguistics and literature. Notice that the answer, and the direction, are not normative, but factual.[27] Our aim is to find some way of organizing the entire enterprise of language studies, a division of labour Lonergan calls a "framework for collaborative creativity."[28] Such a framework would "outline the various clusters of operations to be performed" by language scholars "when they go about their various tasks."[29] "The need for, and pressure towards, that division of labour will become evident as we move forward in the new millennium. The division does not require that one be self luminous: it requires only that one be trapped into respectable performance, much as chemists after the 1860's were trapped into the periodic table."[30]

Language professionals should find the notion of collaboration and division of labour plausible[31] from their sense of specialized estrangement in the field.[32] That such an effort is necessary is evident to those in the field seeking an overview. For whatever people do under the blanket title of language studies, including such things as animal signings, chemical "signatures," computer and cosmic etching, prenatal and early post-natal human gestures – in so far as this data falls under someone's view of language studies, it is grist for the mill of Functional Specialization.

In Functional Specialization, the study of language operates in two distinct phases. Each phase corresponds to one of the operations of the human subject. Therefore, there are eight functional specializations. A first phase of language studies looks to the past, so as to involve four functional specializations: *Research*, *Interpretation*, *History*, and *Dialectic*. A second phase of language studies looks to the future, so there are *Foundations*, *Doctrines*, *Systematics*, and *Communications*. "Next I would like you to consider…the distinction relating to 'looking towards the past' and 'looking towards the future.' Think of the task…the collection and ordering of data, where the ordering is as unobtrusive as possible. Think of library orderings, or even of dictionary orderings, and then notice that the ordering is, as it were, two-faced. You can collect books, fragments, data, in a certain order that you consider convenient for later reading, interpretation, for the question: 'What does this mean?' But that very collecting can have an eye on the future: there can be a desire not just to find out, but to 'get something across.'"[33]

The diagram below shows the correspondence between the operations of the human subject and its intended objects in each phase:

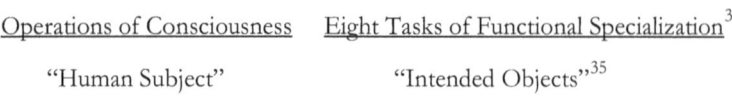

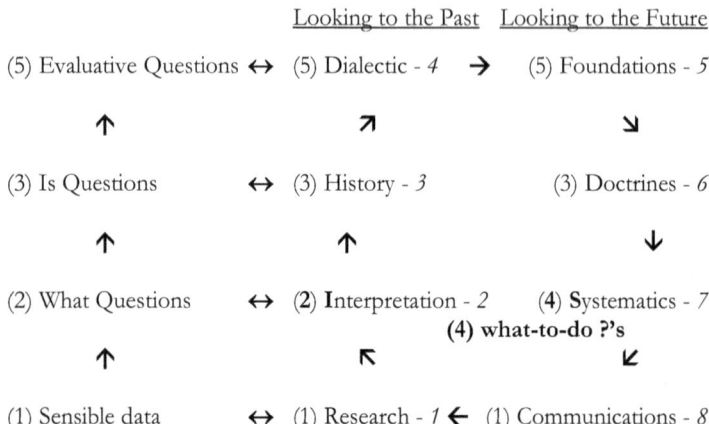

This correspondence yields the following diagram:

R	I	H	D	F	D	S	C
1	2	3	5	5	3	4	1

Notice that there is an asymmetry in the diagram between I-2 and S-4.[36] Please note that while there are four levels in the diagram, there are actually five levels of consciousness. Recall that there are five answers to the question 'Why?' that give one an insightful ordering of causes: material, formal, efficient, exemplary, final. These are related to an order in our consciousness through which one moves from (1) sensible data to (2) what–questions to (3) is-questions to (4) what-to-do questions to (5) evaluative questions: is some-course-of-action worthwhile? Why five levels of consciousness but only eight functional specialties? The big clue to answering that question is in noticing the essential identity of (2) and (4). What makes them different then? Self-attention reveals a basic shift of conscious attitude. For example, one opens the fridge simply to see what is there, and a product wrapped in waxed paper on the shelf prompts the question,

"What might that be?" (I-2) But there is also the possibility of a shift in attitude: one may be intent on producing a meal by asking: "What might that be?" One is then reaching for the idea of a meal, an exemplary cause that will end up becoming approximately the form of the meal (S-4).

Again, appreciation of the asymmetry of I-2 and S-4 may be discovered by engaging in the tricky, long-term task of pondering further on the meaning of a scientific attitude, a "what-orientation," a Wendung zür Idee, or "turn to the idea."[37] The S-4 attitude may ask for possibilities of history, of the incomplete data. In any event, the point is that the what-focus may be for available data in its present form (I-2), OR it may be for data as transformable, the form of which is reached towards through fantasy (S-4).[38]

Here is a listing and brief description of the eight functional specialties that correspond to the five levels of human consciousness and represent the dynamic objects to be sought by investigators in linguistic and literary studies, first, by looking to the past and secondly, by looking to the future:[39]

1. Research: finding relevant data, written or otherwise;
2. Interpretation: reaching the meaning of such data, the meaning of those that produced that data;
3. History: figuring out the story, connecting the meanings of the writings and the doings, etc.;
4. Dialectic: coming up with a best story and the best basic directions;
5. Foundations: expressing the best fundamental (in the sense that they are not tied to age, time, etc.) directions;
6. Doctrines: reaching relevant pragmatic truths, somewhat like the core of national constitutions or of tribal legends;
7. Systematics: drawing correctly and contra-factually on the strategies and discoveries of the past to envisage ranges of time-ordered possibilities.
8. Communications: local collaborative reflection that selects creatively from the ordered ranges of possibilities.

There is a clear delineation amongst the eight tasks. Functional specialization distinguishes and separates successive stages in the process from data to results. Thus, for instance, research aims at determining what was written. The interpreter takes over where the researcher leaves off; her/his aim is to determine what was meant. The historian moves in on a third level; s/he assembles interpreted texts and endeavours to construct a single narrative or view and so on. The main point is that each task involves a different focus, for as Lonergan warns, "functional specialization is essentially not a distinction of specialists but a distinction of specialties. It arises, not to divide the same sort of task among many hands, but to distinguish different tasks and to prevent them from being confused."[40] This distinction is one that emerges spontaneously in the field of language studies. There can be a pretty clear division of labour that distinguishes the accumulation of abundant data from its serious interpretation. The group focused on the accumulation are not distracted by possible significance; the group that tackle interpretation are free from the accumulation problem. Different people with different talents are in each large group, but each group has a definite function: provide the data; provide an interpretation. However, behind these stark distinctions, there are interdependencies: the first group need and use talent in interpretation to provide the data; the second group have competence in the preliminary ordering of data.

We conclude with some brief, but germane, observations. A first feature to notice is that adequacy in "orientation" is central. The problem of organizing that the global community of scholarship in linguistic and literary studies is up against is primarily a problem of method, of procedure. The interest of the global community needs to be an overarching pattern in all the enterprises of language studies. To head toward a definite "perspective," to head toward a precise "orientation," might be to ask in what manner the dynamics of knowing and doing would be found in each task?[41] Whatever the perspective, surely one would grant that the preferred orientation would be an unbiased orientation, whatever that actually means.[42] Sufficient for the moment is to find a pattern implicit in the present work on language and to exploit it creatively in a manner that would both foster richer collaboration and refine the measure of both bias and success in the field. The ordered rolling forward of the creative grinding of language study by Functional Specialization would generate a certain sifting, a survival of the fittest products of creative and reflective data in language studies. We noted above that language professionals should find the notion of collaboration and division of labour a plausible strategy for their field. And so the aim in Chapter 9 will be to reinforce the plausibility of Functional Specialization as a methodological strategy, as well as to introduce how it could be implemented in language studies.

---

¹ Op. cit., *Method*, p. xi.
² Ibid.
³ Op. cit., *The Foundations of Language*, pp. 329-330.
⁴ Paul De Man, *Blindness and Insight*. Oxford University Press, 1971, p. 39.
⁵ Op. cit., *Blindness and Insight*, p. 39.
⁶ In understated fashion, Lonergan wrote, "there is an exigence for further development. There are windows to be opened and fresh air to be let in." Bernard Lonergan, "Christology Today," *A Third Collection: Papers by Bernard J. F. Lonergan, S.J.,* Paulist Press, 1985, p. 89.
⁷ We do not repeat the categories of human desire here since we have already worked them out, along with diagrams, in earlier chapters: the basis of grammatology is the dynamic series of core attitudes, identified as the language universals, formally thematized by Lonergan in Chapter 5.
⁸ It will eventually be called simply "empirical method," the only method that really works.
⁹ "It is at home in the intellectual pattern of experience…supposed and expressed by our account of self-affirmation, of being, and of objectivity. But no man is born into that pattern; no one reaches it easily; no one remains in it permanently; and when some other pattern is dominant, then the self of our self-affirmation seems quite different for one's actual self, the universe of being seems as unreal as Plato's noetic heaven, and objectivity spontaneously becomes a matter of meeting persons and dealing with things that are 'really out there.'" Op. cit., *Insight*, p. 385 [411].
¹⁰ Op. cit., *A Third Collection: Papers by Bernard J. F. Lonergan, S.J.*
¹¹ This illustration first appeared in op. cit., *ICT*, pp. 160-165.
¹² It is important to note that scientists, too, proliferate extra-scientific opinion. An illustration of this fallacy, that parallels the flawed presentation by the writers in Chapter 7, is given in op. cit. *BHT*, pp. 5-6 by McShane: "…what I wish for the beginner in either linguistics or logic is to face that beginning, not truncatedly, but 'head-on.' I would also wish that beginning to be not just head-on, but hearty, wholesome. Immediately I must note that **I cannot tell you what that means**. And this brings me to the deeper negative element in culture that is even less **tellable**: It is a topic that is tied into the meaning of my strange title [*A Brief History of Tongue: From Big Bang To Coloured Wholes*], and so it is best to comment immediately on the origin of that title. Perhaps you have already caught on to the echo of Stephen Hawking's *A Brief History of*

Time. From the Big Bang to Black Holes in the title of my book. There is a parallel interest in the presentation of foundational physics, but there is a deep conflict regarding **tellability**. Attention to some of Hawking's introductory remarks can help to focus elementary reflections. 'Where did the universe come from? How and why did it begin? Will it come to an end, and if so, how? These are questions that are of interest to us all. But modern science has become so technical that only a small number of specialists are able to master the mathematics used to describe them. Yet the basic ideas about the origin and fate of the universe can be stated without mathematics in a form that people without a scientific education can understand.'" See op. cit., *ICT*, Chapter 42, "Physics," pp. 170-174.

[13] See ibid., "Chapter 38, Psychology and Ethics," pp. 151-156.

[14] These attitudes permeate all levels and disciplines of education. "My popular pointing here recalls a remark made...about physics being the most elementary science. The [fallacious] expectation is that it is the most difficult, tackled only by the smartest students. Chemistry is obviously easier; if you have a decent memory you can manage botany; almost anyone can mess with fruitflies and frogs: and if you are really not at all bright you could still get by in areas like psychology, sociology, religious studies. The [fallacious] expectation has reality upside down: the result is a 'heading off of *nomos*, so that, for instance, one can cynically talk of sociology as the science where people count." Op. cit., *BHT*, p. 128.

[15] Aristotle, *Poetics*, 1456^b 1, 23-4.

[16] This process has implications for the meaning of adult growth. I would direct readers to various chapters in *ICT* for an introductory account of those implications. In the context of Botany and Zoology, Chapters 44 and 45 in particular open up the topic of adult growth in a manner we begin to intimate here as the procedure of GEM: "What is this adult growth and what might drive it? We are back with Aristotle...Adult growth is wonder let loose by an ethos of encouragement, by the cultivation of questing in all zones of human interest....Then the sunflower's growth is possessed in the little non-space of our human minding, and can become slowly over a lifetime, part of that larger growth, the growth of the universe of mind, and the growth of the mind minding the mind's growing: what we have been attempting as beginners here....a new ethos, a new integral perspective on the amazing solution to the problem of living that is the human thing." Op. cit., *ICT*, pp. 182-183 and 188.

[17] "Then the rhythms of all the human tongues of history are no longer tied to touch-sight-taste-tone but find their place, along with traces of ancient radiations, in an aggreformic emergentist heuristic of our material finitude." Op. cit., *BHT*, p. 119. This is true whether the word be densely referential – op. cit., *Ulysses*' (p. 32) "contranmagnificandjewbangtantiality" - or, like "the," singularly pale, even as it concludes *Finnegan's Wake*. A metaphysics of words, of language relates an aggreformic function $W(pi,cj,bk,zl)$ to functions $F(pi,cj,bk,zl,um,rn)$ within the integral perspective of $HSf(pi,cj,bk,zl,um,rn)$. That relating meshes into the reality of "the finality of intellect" (op. cit.,

Insight, p.xxii [16]), that "all we know is somehow with us" (ibid., p. 278 [303]), that "every consistent choice, at least implicitly, is a choice of universal order". (ibid., p.605 [629]).

[18] William Wordsworth, "Ode: Intimations of Immortality From Recollections of Early Childhood," I, Op. cit., *Norton*, p. 176.

[19] This topic is treated more fully in John Benton, "Lonergan and the Meaning of Word," *Journal of Macrodynamic Analysis*, (4) 2004, a Website journal: www.mun.ca/jmda.

[20] See op. cit., *Insight*, p. 464 [489]. "Study of the organism begins from the thing-for-us, from the organism as exhibited to our senses...."

[21] Op. cit., *Method*, p. 260.

[22] Op. cit., *BHT*, p. 114. The reader could follow up on this topic further in the chapter "Thoughts, Tongues and Times: The Drive of Foundations," pp. 111-137.

[23] Op. cit., *Method*, p. 70.

[24] Op. cit., *BHT*, p. 125.

[25] A more detailed description of the tasks may be found in ibid., 125-145. In op. cit., *BHT*, McShane presents the topic under in the chapter, "A Rolling Stone Gathers *Nomos*," pp. 80-107. We draw from that chapter in this section.

[26] Patrick Kavanagh, *The Complete Poems of Patrick Kavanagh*. New York: Hand Press, 1972, p. 288. From the poem titled, "To Hell With Commonsense."

[27] Our notion of the term "normative" relates to core grammar as follows, "The detached and disinterested desire to know and its unfolding in inquiry and reflection not only constitute a notion of being but also impose a normative structure upon man's cognitional acts. Such a structure provides the relations by which unknown content of the acts can be defined heuristically. This heuristic structure is immanent and operative in all knowing [and doing]. Op. cit., *Insight*, pp. 395-396 [420].

[28] Op. cit., *Method*, p. xi.

[29] Ibid.

[30] Op. cit., *BHT*, p. 115.

[31] This notion of plausibility gives rise to my use of the expression "shadow zones" in Chapter 9. Why shadow zones? They represent the starting point that distinguishes present cultural conditions from future cultural conditions for Functional Specialization and its manifold complexity. One complexity assumes that GEM is occurring in all the specialties. Further complexities are raised by Lonergan in Op. cit., *Method*, pp. 249-250, especially the desperate need for theoretic displacement, the lack of which occupied our attention in Chapter 7. As Butterfield observes, the natural drive toward theoretic displacement has been replaced by extra-scientific opinion in most disciplines. Moreover, there are further related complexities, long-neglected by present cultural conditions, specified by Lonergan in two key passages: "These issues can be skirted or evaded....But [language studies] can be methodical only if these issues are met head on. To meet them head on is the problem of our fourth specialty, dialectic" (Ibid., pp. 248-9) "If categories are to be derived,

there is needed a base from which they are derived...the basic nest of terms and relations [our grounding language universals]. Further, the basic nest of terms and relations can be differentiated in a number of manners....Such differentiation vastly enriches he initial nest of terms and relations. From such a broadened basis one can go on to a developed account of the human good, values, beliefs, to the carriers, elements, functions, realms, and stages of meaning, to the question of God, of religious experience its expression, its dialectical development." (Ibid., pp. 285-287)

[32] Given the plethora of data in the field of language studies, its diversity, and its relentless expansion, it is clear that adventurous "Lone Rangers" and "rugged individualists," however gifted, who attempt to do every task that is required to promote progress in this field, relegate their efforts, at best, to the marginalized status of the "gifted amateur," and at worst, to the ever-increasing and immense manifold of random data. This topic is pursued further in Chapter 9.

[33] Op. cit., *BHT*, p. 85. "As a clear illustration of eyeing the future, consider present concerns with phonology and with written linguistic expression. Even without knowledge of the field, you cannot help but notice, I hope, the two faces, or what is better designated as two phases of reflective concern with data. One can focus on the ordering of tongue and script in available languages; one can focus on control of expression that looks to the future of reading, writing, education, communication, and indeed, (this should give you pause), on the ordering that will help the future control of investigations of linguistics."

[34] See Op. cit., *BHT*, p. 98. The names assigned to each specialty are not etched in stone; indeed, some may need to be modified to suit language studies. The numbers in parentheses denote the correspondence between the levels of human consciousness and the functional tasks. The order of consciousness shows that one moves from (1) sensible data to (2) what-questions to (3) is-questions to (4) what-to-do questions to (5) evaluative questions: "is some-course-of-action worthwhile?" The numbers in italics denote the numerical order of the eight functional tasks.

[35] One may be helped by the image of a vortex, a continuous whirl of tasks. Note in the first diagram above the direction of the arrows under "Intended Objects" indicates the continuous forward movement of a wheel. The "twist" I add here is that the tasks move not in a linear fashion, but in spiral fashion, to indicate symbolically, an upwardly mobile "vortex" of "cumulative and progressive results."

[36] The asymmetry is indicated by the bolding of numbers "I2" and "S4" in the diagram.

[37] Appreciating this asymmetry reinforces the fact that curiosity about core invariant question structures is worth a much larger focus in the field of language study, and "that not just the linguistic expressions, but the subjective realities to which they refer, are at the heart of understanding human language." (Ibid., p. 99) The beginning of a scientific attitude can be captured

in the statement: one cannot give or acquire an appreciation by giving and receiving a definition: one needs to appeal to experience.

[38] The diagram of op. cit., *Method*, p.48, can be a help here in envisaging "capacity" and its relation to the massive transposition of the "institution " of language that needs to be fantasized. For an elementary introduction see op. cit., *ICT*, Chapter 31, "Conversations," pp. 119-123. Also, see Philip McShane, *The Shaping of the Foundations*, University Press of America, 1977, pp. 97-118. In Chapter Four McShane introduces the notion of "fantasy" as a serious heuristic attitude. "What is important is the raising, with some precision and fantasy, of the question of the need for symbol and diagram to control and expand the methodology of on-going process. Some such mesh of symbols would broaden the perspective of the dialectician towards a more massive effective and affective retrieval, and open the foundational…possibilities of objectifying elements relevant to the last three specialities." (p. 117) The focus of Welleck and Warren and Greenberg and Rutherford might suggest an imbalance of methodologies "looking to the past" as opposed to methodologies "looking to the future." And yet, on closer inspection, their orientation actually parallels my effort here to fantasize forward toward the possibility of a minute transformative shift in the systematics of the academy's daily doings in historical process by raising the question, "What is to be done?" Hence the use of "symbol and diagram to control and expand the methodology of on-going process." Similarly, the symbolic reference to the metaphor "rolling stones" in Kavanagh's poem at the beginning of this section is suggestive of the dynamic "wheel" of human creativity and human reflection on creativity contemporarily encrusted by the "moss" of oversight concerning the existence, meaning and implications of the data of quest, and its offspring, the stagnant orientation wrought by the dominant cultural heritage of "extra-scientific" opinion. Hence, "[n]othing thought out / atones for no flight / in the light." In the alternative, Functional Specialization grounded by GEM, is a liberating strategy of efficient "flight in the light."

[39] For a fuller description I would direct the reader at once to the chapter "A Rolling Stone Gathers *Nomos*," op. cit., *ICT*, pp. 80-110. McShane shows how linguistic data would apply to each specialty. The examples are of immediate interest to language professionals. For a more general audience, I would highly recommend a story that would be "helpful in discovering the homeliness of function specialization. The story is of a Toronto family that has a holiday cottage at some lake north of the city." Ibid., pp. 101-104.

[40] See Op. cit., *Method*, p. 136.

[41] Here it would be profitable to go back to the beginning of the chapter and reflect on the illustration and exercise of how GEM would be implemented in language studies.

[42] For enlargement on the meaning of bias, see op. cit., *Insight*, pp. 191-206 [214-31] and 218-225 [244-50].

9

TOWARDS METHODOLOGICAL RESTRUCTURING IN LANGUAGE STUDIES

The purpose of this chapter is to support and reinforce the acceptability and plausibility of the methodological strategy, Functional Specialization, introduced in Chapter 8. My approach is empirical, an orientation of which I call "methodological heuristics." First, I provide evidence of the need for restructuring in language studies with a survey of journals that spontaneously identifies various 'shadow'[1] zones of specialties and reveals evidence of a collective lack of vision for a way to control the growing amount of literary and linguistic meaning. Secondly, I survey one journal, in a manner that provides a framework for critical reflection, through a detailed analysis of the evidence that invites Functional Specialization. Thirdly, in the last two sections of this chapter, I provide further evidence that again spontaneously identifies the various 'shadow' zones of tasks discussed in random fashion by proponents representing literary and linguistic studies; primarily, I will be referring both to appeals, as well as to empirical data conducive to procedural restructuring, that spontaneously anticipate Functional Specialization, made respectively by Welleck and Warren in literary studies, and by Greenberg and Rutherford in linguistic studies.

1. A Survey of Journals in Language Studies

A focused survey of ten major journals representing the spectrum of scholarship in the field of language studies provides an enlightening microcosm of spontaneity, randomness and fragmentation that draws attention to a lack of unity and efficiency in a publishing community focused on field specialization as opposed to functional specialization. Each journal declares its mandate. Furthermore, its contributors undertake what appears to me to be a randomness of tasks.

1. "Recent *Americanist* scholarship has generated some of the most forceful responses to questions about literary history and theory. Yet too many of the most provocative essays have been scattered among a wide variety of narrowly focused publications. [There is needed a] forum for the various, often competing voices of contemporary literary inquiry."[2]
2. "*Essays in Criticism* covers the whole field of English Literature from the time of Chaucer to the present day. The journal maintains that originality in interpretation must be allied to the best scholarly standards.[3] Moreover, whilst always pursuing new directions and responding to new developments, *Essays in Criticism* has kept a balance between the constructive and the skeptical, giving the journal particular value at a time when criticism has become so diversified."[4]
3. "*The Cambridge Quarterly* was established on, and remains committed to, the principle that literature is an art, and that the purpose of art is to give pleasure and enlightenment. The journal devotes itself principally to literary criticism and its fundamental aim to take a critical look at accepted views."[5]
4. "*Forum for Modern Language Studies* has published articles on all aspects of literary and linguistic studies, from the Middle Ages to the present day. The journal sets out to reflect the essential pluralism of modern language and literature studies and to provide a forum for worldwide scholarly discussion."[6]
5. "*Literary and Linguistic Computing* is an international journal which publishes…research projects, description and evaluation of techniques and methodologies, and reports on work in progress."[7]
6. "*Literature and Theology* provides a forum for interdisciplinary dialogue, inviting both close textual analysis and broader theoretical speculation as ways of exploring how religion is embedded within culture. Contributions, addressing questions of interest to both the disciplines of literature and theology, are encouraged to confront and challenge traditional modes of discourse within a wide range of related fields, encompassing biblical criticism, literary criticism, philosophy, politics, history, cultural studies, and contemporary critical

theory or practice."[8]
7. "[T]he primary intention of *Notes and Queries* is devoted principally to English language and literature, lexicography, history, and scholarly antiquarianism. Each issue focuses on the works of a particular period, with an emphasis on the factual rather than the speculative. The journal comprises notes, book reviews, readers' queries and replies."[9]
8. "*The Review of English Studies* [emphasizes] historical scholarship rather than interpretive criticism, though fresh evaluation of writers and their work are also offered in the light of newly discovered or existing material."[10]
9. "*The Year's Work in English Studies* is the qualitative narrative bibliographical review of scholarly work on English language and literatures written in English. Each volume includes a detailed overview from Old English to contemporary critical works for a given year, and contains critical notices for some 1100 books; extensive coverage of English Language, American Literature, New Literatures in English and English Literature; coverage of specialist periodicals; comprehensive indexing by critic, author, and subject; plus bibliographical endnotes for each chapter."[11]
10. "*Journal of Linguistics* is concerned with all branches of theoretical linguistics, including syntax, morphology, phonology, phonetics, semantics, pragmatics and historical, sociological, computational, psychological, literary and applied aspects of language and linguistic theory."[12]

Significantly, and in so many words that imply an absence of efficiency, the declarations of the various journals listed here observe that there is a lack of communal purpose and goal to the overall enterprise in their field of study. Also significant is a stunning sense of innocence behind the sentiment that a single journal could presume to possess the capacity for a comprehensive "control of meaning" of that which is clearly an unimaginably complex manifold of creative and reflective data. Moreover, there is the compactness of commonsense spontaneity, first, in the healthy acknowledgement of fragmentation in "competing voices" scattered "among a wide variety of narrowly focused publications," in an environment in which "criticism has become so diversified;" secondly, but not so healthy, is the vast range of foci, the shadows of the specialties, that appear not only within a journal itself, but within various parts of each article.[13] Finally, fundamentally absent is a forward-looking acknowledgement of the need for a luminously collective procedure that would parallel Functional Specialization: an overarching pattern in linguistic and literary scholarship that would invite richer collaboration and refine the measure of both bias and success by the ordered rolling forward of the creative grinding of both; by generating a certain sifting, toward a survival of the fittest products, both creative and reflective, with the proximate goal of progress in the field, and the distant goal of gradually transforming human culture.

In brief, for all the richness and diversity of data within the medium, the stakeholders lack a practical mandate grounded by a strategy committed to addressing the need for an efficient globally collective procedure with which to structure that richness and diversity in a manner that would yield cumulative and progressive results.

2. Anticipating Methodological Restructuring in Language Studies

This part of the chapter points ahead to the final two sections to indicate the impossible task of critically analyzing the foregoing journals in their complex manifold of creative and reflective data. In this section I offer a paradigm for, and sense of, an efficient heuristic of critical reflection that could emerge. I do so by illustrating the possibility and plausibility for a comprehensive "control of meaning" that would anticipate the emergence of Functional Specialization.[14] I take as my example a plethora of reflective data from the literary journal, *The Cambridge Quarterly*.[15] In the first group of samples in "Part A," a description for each of the original articles reveals shadows of the specialties embedded in the listing.[16] The second sample in "Part B," reveals the shadows of the specialties within various parts of one article in a detailed empirical study of "Englands of the Mind," by David Gervais.

First, I briefly review the strategic framework for Functional Specialization. From this review, one is then in a position to notice the shadows occurring spontaneously of one or more of the specialties. Because I am dealing with a journal of literary studies, I describe the specialties with that context in mind.

Literary studies may be divided into two distinct phases: a first phase, looking to the past, and a second phase, looking to the future. In looking to the past, there is a first specialty, *Research*, that uncovers and makes available the relevant data, written or otherwise; there is a second specialty, *Interpretation*, that understands the meaning of such data as well as the meaning of those who produced that data; there is a third specialty, *History*, that judges and narrates what occurred by figuring out the story, connecting the meanings of the writings and the doings. It goes beyond the meaning of individual works to seek out the patterns of literary advance, patterns of which reveal emergent literary doctrines; the labour of the first phase culminates with a fourth specialty, *Dialectics*, that seeks to thematize the basis of evaluation and of progress by working toward an improvement of orientation. In so doing, Dialectic endeavors to unravel the conflicts concerning values, fact, meanings, and experiences. It aims to bring forth grounded foundations for the task of criticism by engaging in what might be referred to as a criticism of criticism.[17] In effect, it is wisdom looking to the past by specialists who seek the foundations of past success and point towards orientations and methodologies beneficial to the future.

In looking to the future, there is a fifth specialty, *Foundations*, which, in effect, is wisdom facing the future. The specialist in foundations possesses a heuristic open invariant vision of the future of language, linguistics and literature that expresses the best fundamental (in the sense that they are not tied to age, time, etc.) directions;[18] there is a sixth specialty, *Doctrines*, that reaches relevant pragmatic truths, somewhat like the core of national constitutions or of tribal legends. The issue of literary genres and the principles implicit in their creation and reception falls within this specialty. It parallels the historical task by engaging in the effort to bring forth principles of creativity and response; there is a seventh specialty, *Systematics*, that seeks an integral understanding of such principles; the labour of the second phase culminates with the specialty, *Communications*, from which emerges local collaborative reflection that selects creatively from the ordered ranges of possibilities making the fruits of these principles accessible to concrete literary experience. Moreover, I would note that while the fourth level tasks, Dialectics and Foundations, are integral searchings for foundations of progress, the other tasks are more precisely focused on the conventionally recognizable interests in literary studies.

What precisely is this journal doing? The mandate quoted above reflects shadows of the specialties: "*The Cambridge Quarterly* was established on, and remains committed to, the principle that literature is an art, and that the purpose of art is to give pleasure and enlightenment. The journal devotes itself principally to literary criticism and its fundamental aim to take a critical look at accepted views."[19] The shadow of *doctrines* is reflected by its commitment to a truth based on a spontaneous stand on "principle" with respect to the existence and purpose of "art" and "literature." The shadow of *dialectics* is reflected by "its fundamental aim to take a critical look at accepted views," with a spontaneous stand on "enlightenment" loosely akin to a "criticism of criticism." It is also worth noticing the random juxtaposition of these two specialties in the declaration.

Part A

The four samples below are analyzed again, this time by asking the methodological question: "what precisely is the writer doing?" From this review, there emerge the 'shadows' of a number of specialties, randomly placed, not only within the journal listings, but also within various parts of the articles themselves.[20]

In the article, "Henry James's *Bostonians*: The Voices of Democracy,"[21] Jean Gooder interprets and evaluates James's novel with the aim to identify and move toward the "true nature" of a collective democratic voice. By engaging in *interpretation* the author expresses an understanding of the meaning of the creative data (*Bostonians*) as well as an understanding of the meaning of the author who produced the data (James). By engaging in a *dialectical* evaluation of the novel and of its creator, the author endeavors to discredit "post-modern" orientation concerning reflection on values, fact, meanings, and experiences in the creator and his product, with an orientation underpinned by a spontaneous assumption about the meaning of "soul," "intellect," and "nature." By venturing into the realm of the expression of the "true nature" of a collective democratic voice, the author reflects on relevant pragmatic truths such as would be associated with the specialty, *doctrines*.

In the article, "DeLillo's Libra and the Real,"[22] Stuart Hutchinson evaluates various "post-modern" interpretations of DeLillo's novel, *Libra*, with the aim to establish the truth of the novel's actual meaning. The author reflects on the truth of the novel's actual meaning by expressing his own *interpretation*. Moreover, the author draws on spontaneous criteria to judge the novel's "actual" meaning and the relevance of the story's meaning to actual events in *history*. By engaging in a *dialectical* evaluation of a variety of "post-modern" interpretations, both of the novel and of the doing of its creator, the author endeavors to resolve conflicts concerning values, facts, meanings, and experiences in the creator and his product, with an orientation underpinned by a spontaneous assumption about the meaning of "the Real."

In the article, "D. H. Lawrence as Verse Translator,"[23] David Cram and Christopher Pollnitz investigate the history of Lawrence's various translations, and judge the originality of his translations with the aim to evaluate him as a translator. The authors engage in *research* to uncover the relevant written data, original and otherwise, that Lawrence either created or drew on to write his translations. The authors connect the meanings of both Lawrence's writings and doings to produce a *historical* account from which he could be evaluated as an original translator. By engaging in a *dialectical* evaluation of the translator's method, the authors take a stand on allegations of error and dishonesty in Lawrence's work from which to spontaneously judge its ultimate effect on the value of his translations.

In the article, "Englands of the Mind,"[24] David Gervais seeks first, to understand, secondly, to establish facticity, and thirdly to evaluate a variety of responses to the question, "[w]hat exactly does 'Englishness' mean and why is it important?". In raising this question, the author heads toward issues that extend to the specialties *interpretation*, *history*, and *dialectic*. The author engages in *interpretive* activity by reflecting on the meaning of the expression

"Englishness" as it has been treated within England's literary tradition by both creative and reflective sources. Furthermore, the author engages in *historical* activity by laboring to figure out the story, to connect the meanings of the writings that would ground the existence of the culture, "Englishness." Moreover, the author proceeds with *dialectical* activity by contrasting the vision of creative and reflective sources that explore cultural identity in England and France respectively. Moreover, there is a complex interlocking of *dialectical* and *foundational* dialogue that hints at a need for a "methodology" by transposing the question of its importance (viz. its value), from the context of looking toward the past for wisdom, to focusing on the context of future wisdom for solutions to the question. The complexity with which the question is treated is increased manifold by the author's spontaneous assumption of the meaning of "empiricism," "self-criticism," "ideology," "metaphysics;" this spontaneous orientation toward both past and future wisdom in the search for solutions to problems is reinforced by the dialogue, "something we carry in our minds," "the way we think about it," "the sense we have of ourselves."[25] Furthermore, a heuristic methodological vision for "progress" is foreshadowed by the author's observation that the topic "provoked so much introspection in us. But writers who chart this debate...need a larger context for what they say to have any general resonance...it is a case of by indirections finding directions out;"[26] "The 'lost traveler's dream under the hill' lies in the future, not in the past."[27] Finally, the study shows evidence of activity related to *doctrines* when the author implies that a principle on which the genuine meaning of "Englishness" may be founded would run parallel to that by which Eliot wrote of Virgil: "'Virgil made of Roman civilization something better than it really was.'"[28]

Part B

The following analysis focuses on patterns of procedure that reveal shadows of the specialties in various parts of the article "Englands of the Mind," by David Gervais. The reader should notice a random shifting amongst shadow specialties between paragraphs, between sentences within a paragraph, and between groups of words within a sentence.

Sample Paragraph 1

[1] The English have usually been seen as a nation of doers rather than thinkers. [2] Unlike the French, their national policy has been founded on expediency rather than ideas. [3] 'England' has rarely been an abstraction as 'La France' was to Napoleon or Louis XIV. [4] Even Cromwell was guided in the last resort by pragmatism. [5] There is no English equivalent for an adventure like Napoleon's Russian campaign, where policy was subdued to imperial ideology. [6] At times, the 'roast-beef of old England' has fulfilled the same symbolic function as the mantra 'Liberté, Egalité, Fraternité' has in France. [7] Not only do the English resist articulating their 'Englishness,' they feel truer to themselves by not articulating it. [8] An English quatorze juillet is hard to imagine. [9] Thus, late Victorian imperialism seems a hothouse growth, British rather than English. [10] 'Englishness' is less blatant, a half-private feeling held in common, too instinctive for public affirmation. [11] It derives from landscape and poetry (especially Shakespeare's) more than from pride in political institutions. [12] An English Versailles is inconceivable. [13] The King James Bible has done more to foster a common consciousness than King James and all his successors have. [14] Dickens, the most English of writers, rhapsodized about the English countryside but caricatured Parliament as a long-running farce. [15] Countless English patriots still share his prejudice.[29]

Methodological Analysis of Sample Paragraph 1

The first sentence makes a judgment about England's story (history). The second sentence makes an evaluative judgment between the truth of England's story and the truth of France's story (dialectic). The third sentence expresses the judgement that the "idea" of "England" is not analogous to that of "France" (dialectic). The fourth sentence interprets the motives of Cromwell (interpretation). The fifth sentence interprets the strategy behind Napoleon's Russian campaign (interpretation) and judges that a parallel policy does not exist in England's history (doctrines). The sixth sentence interprets English symbolism (interpretation) and makes a comparative judgment between English symbolism and French symbolism (dialectic). The seventh sentence meshes an interpretation of English "self image" (interpretation) with a forward-looking evaluation that would ground a fundamental truth: "feel truer to themselves" (foundations). The eighth sentence denies the existence of a symbol similar to the date of July 14th in France as having a parallel meaning for England (doctrines). The ninth sentence interprets Victorian "self image" (interpretation). The tenth sentence asserts a time-tested truth about contemporary English culture (doctrines). The eleventh sentence interprets the meaning of contemporary reflection on English "self image" (interpretation). The twelfth sentence parallels the eighth sentence by denying the existence of a symbol similar to that of Versailles in France as having a parallel meaning for England (doctrines). The thirteenth sentence asserts that the King James Bible is a symbol for "common consciousness" (doctrines); it also makes a judgment about the meaning of King James himself (history) and about the collective meaning of his followers (history). The fourteenth sentence interprets the meaning of Dickens (interpretation). The fifteenth sentence evaluates the collective contemporary attitude of "countless English patriots" (dialectic).

Sample Paragraph 2

[1] But even on these terms, 'Englishness' is hardly enough on its own. [2] Montesquieu once said 'Je suis homme d'être français'. [3] English art has to be more than just English. [4] To think of Purcell as an 'English composer,' as if that were to distinguish him from Bach or Monteverdi, is to obscure the music. [5] The English like to think of Shakespeare as 'English' but, to the rest of the world, his plays are simply drama itself. [6] Great art has a nationality of its own. [7] If we link its meaning to its origins we risk confusing it with politics. [8] Cultural studies and culture is not the same thing. [9] Is Goethe any less German for discovering part of himself through Shakespeare? [10] When Charles V picked up Titian's brush or when the evangelical Ruskin was bowled over by the counter-Reformation allegories of the Scuola di San Rocco, they were acknowledging that ideology is more finite than art. [11] Yet a

great deal of English art, even that of a major figure like Britten, can seem over-conscious of its own 'Englishness.' [12] Geoffrey Hill matters because he is able to express the experience of 'Englishness' through the experience of the rest of Europe. [13] (The English poets of the great war seem to be writing about an English war.) [14] Even Kipling asked, 'What do they know of England who only England know?' [15] Being set in a silver sea has its drawbacks. Sometimes writers need to leave home. [16] The problem for them today is that Europe, let alone the world, offers them only a politico-economic destination not a cultural one.[30]

Methodological Analysis of Sample Paragraph 2

The first sentence evaluates the limitations of the meaning of "Englishness" (dialectic). The second sentence interprets Montesquieu (interpretation). The third sentence expresses a heuristic openness to the truth about English art (foundations). The fourth sentence interprets the meaning of Purcell, Bach and Monteverdi (interpretation); it also implies a principle by which a composer would be judged (doctrines). The fifth sentence interprets the meaning of Shakespeare, the English people, the world at large (interpretation); it also implies a principle by which dramatic art would be judged (doctrines). The sixth sentence asserts a principle about art (doctrines). The seventh sentence interprets the meaning of art (interpretation) and meshes this interpretation with an evaluation of the meaning of politics (dialectic). The ninth sentence interprets the meaning of "cultural studies" and "culture" (interpretation). The tenth sentence interprets the meaning of Charles V and Ruskin (interpretation); it also attributes to their doings a principle about art (doctrines). The eleventh sentence interprets the meaning of Britten (interpretation). The twelfth sentence interprets the meaning of Hill (interpretation). The thirteenth sentence interprets the meaning of the poets of the "Great War" (interpretation). The use of a rhetorical question by Kipling in the fourteenth sentence implies an interpretation of the meaning of Kipling (interpretation). The fifteenth sentence hypothesizes about the intrinsic needs of writers in order to function properly as artists (systematics). The sixteenth sentence offers a perspective, looking to the past, on the culture in which writers are working (dialectic).

Sample Paragraph 3

[1] Yet even an entrenched 'Englishness' has been less rampant than one might have expected. [2] Even since Arnold and Henry James tried to diagnose 'British culture,' the subject has been veiled in irony. [3] In E.M. Forster, for instance, irony is so pervasive that it turns into a mannerism. [4] We meet it in more exacting forms in writers such as T. S. Eliot and Geoffrey Hill, whenever England is at issue. [5] Each instinctively feels that to tackle the subject head-on would be not just unsubtle but reckless – a recipe for priggishness. [6] Even with abundant irony, Arnold sometimes fell into that trap. [7] 'Culture,' as a thing in itself, is a minefield. [8] Coupled with the word 'English,' it seems either an oxymoron or a pretext for boasting. [9] The English often praise Shakespeare as if he were a sort of intellectual standing army. [10] 'Culture' craves wary walking. [11] In practice, expatriate Americans like James and Eliot manage this better than the English themselves do. [12] The writers who have been most serious about England – Ruskin, Lawrence, F.R. Leavis – are often too gripped by their own prophecies or too hectoring or sectarian to be 'cultured' themselves. [13] Arnold never doubted Ruskin's sincerity, but he felt that it made him too Hebraic to do justice to culture's Hellenic bent. [14] One may grant this objection even if, like me, one thinks Ruskin a greater critic than Arnold was. [15] Eliot, who had scores to settle with Arnold, at once saw how much a modern critic needed irony. [16] He saw, not least, how vital it was to any critic, like himself, who had pontificating of his own to do. [17] Hence his dogmatic insistence on classicism, the 'European mind,' and the 'prose virtues,' all intended as antidotes to Hebraic (and Romantic) certainty. [18] The many English writers, Leavis included, who were in Eliot's debt saw a similar reserve as a condition of their own modernity. [19] Only such a weapon could resist the solemn inheritance of the Victorians. [20] Lytton Strachey's irony may seem simplistic now but it is a useful barometer of the distance the English needed to keep from their own 'Englishness.'[31]

Methodological Analysis of Sample Paragraph 3

The first sentence makes a judgment about the impact of the culture named "Englishness" (history). The second sentence interprets the meaning of Arnold and James; it also interprets the tone in which that meaning is expressed (interpretation). The third sentence interprets the meaning of Forster; it also interprets the tone in which that meaning is expressed (interpretation). The fourth sentence interprets the meaning of Eliot and Hill; it also interprets the tone in which that meaning is expressed (interpretation). The fifth sentence makes a judgment about the meaning of Eliot and Hill (history). The sixth sentence makes a judgment about the meaning of Arnold (history). The seventh sentence makes a judgement about the meaning of human culture (history). The eighth sentence evaluates the meaning of the "idea" of culture in contrast to the meaning of the "idea" of "English" (dialectic). The ninth sentence interprets the meaning of Shakespeare and the collective meaning of the English public (interpretation). The tenth sentence hypothesizes about the proper function of cultural interpretation (systematics). The eleventh sentence evaluates the reflections of James and Eliot (dialectic); it also holds the reflections of James and Eliot up as exemplars that anticipate the proper function of cultural interpretation (systematics). The twelfth sentence evaluates the meaning of Ruskin, Lawrence and Leavis as well as the meaning of their reflections (dialectic). The thirteenth sentence evaluates the opposing perspectives of Arnold and Ruskin (dialectic). The fourteenth sentence judges the superiority of Ruskin's perspective as a cultural critic over Arnold's (dialectic). The fifteenth sentence evaluates the opposing perspectives of Eliot and Arnold (dialectic). The sixteenth sentence interprets the meaning of Eliot (interpretation). The seventeenth sentence acknowledges the validity of principles for cultural criticism embraced by Eliot (doctrines); it also evaluates opposing principles: "classicism" versus "Hebraic" and "Romantic" (dialectic). The eighteenth sentence judges the English literary tradition as a whole, and Leavis in particular, as holding to the principles embraced by Eliot (history). The nineteenth sentence judges the cultural tone (suggestive of principles) embraced by the "Victorians" (history). The twentieth sentence judges the meaning of Strachey's tone toward cultural criticism (history).

 This exercise in methodological heuristics continues in the final two sections with the random and spontaneous anticipations first, of Welleck and Warren in literary studies, and secondly, of Greenberg and Rutherford in linguistic studies. These add further plausibility to the need for Functional Specialization in the field of language study.

3. Anticipating Functional Specialization in Literary Studies

In *Theory of Literature*, Welleck and Warren anticipate the need for Functional Specialization in literary study. In the introduction, they state that their goal is "to provide an *organon* of method."[32] In random and spontaneous fashion, they specify various facets that loosely parallel, in a shadowy manner, some of the specialties. I list those facets in a way that point toward the basic ordering of the specialties found in Functional Specialization.

1. "research" – In Part Two, Chapter Six, entitled "The Ordering and Establishing of Evidence,"[33] they indicate the need for preliminary operations of establishing and ordering texts.
2. "interpretation" – In Part Four, there is what they call "the intrinsic study of the literary work," of what the literary work means. Chapter Twelve deals with "The Mode of Existence of a Literary Work of Art,"[34] Chapter Thirteen discusses "Euphony, Rhythm and Metre,"[35] Chapter Fifteen explores "Image, Metaphor, Symbol, Myth."[36] Furthermore, they provide a sufficient indication of the strategies of this stage in Chapter Six for both the texts of creativity and the texts of response.
3. "history" – They indicate the need for a historical dimension that builds on the first two. In Chapter Nineteen, "Literary History," they point to the need to go beyond the meaning of individual works to seek out the patterns of literary advance to reveal emergent literary doctrines.[37]
4. "dialectics" – In the chapter "Evaluation," Welleck and Warren acknowledge that the concrete achievements of these tasks may not be uniform. For example, the history may be Marxist, the interpretation structuralist;[38] hence, there is the dimension of evaluation that would best fulfil the quest commensurate with R.S. Crane's search for a criticism of

criticism.[39]
5. "foundations" – What Welleck and Warren list under "The extrinsic approach to the study of literature"[40] might be more properly considered a set of mediations that would ground a perspective on mediating the literary activities of the future. Such a set of mediations is foreshadowed by topics covered in the chapters "Literature and Psychology,"[41] "Literature and Society,"[42] "Literature and Ideas,"[43] and "Literature and the Other Arts."[44]
6. "doctrines" – In Chapter Seventeen, "Literary Genres,"[45] Welleck and Warren identify the problem of literary genres and the principles implicit in their creation and reception; this anticipates the need to bring forth principles of creativity and response that would parallel the historical task.
7. "systematics" – Welleck and Warren acknowledge "[t]he old methods…are and must be reviewed and restated in modern terms. New methods based on a survey of the wider range of forms in modern literature are being introduced."[46] There is the need for some coherent account of these principles within a systematic task that seeks an integral understanding of such principles.
8. "communications" – There is too, the task of making the fruits of these principles accessible to concrete literary experience with a final task that mediates the concrete transformation of creativity and response. Welleck and Warren raise the issue of a renewed search for "the natural and sensible starting-point for work in literary scholarship,"[47] while acknowledging, "a healthy reaction has taken place which recognizes that the study of literature should… [cut] across the old boundary lines."[48]

4. Anticipating Functional Specialization in Linguistic Studies[49]

In *Universals of Human Language* (UHL), Greenberg anticipates the need for Functional Specialization, and along with Rutherford in *Language Universals and Second Language Acquisition* (LU), exhibits the shadows of the specialties in various parts of the articles in his volume of studies. In his introduction to the first volume, Greenberg pushes for a radical methodological overhaul citing as the point of departure the need to focus on "matters of fundamental significance…to contribute a more general perspective – historical, methodological, and interdisciplinary – to the work as a whole…if linguistics [is] to progress as a science…."[50] Rutherford concludes the introduction of his volumes by quoting Comrie's essay: "the literature has pointed to a number of ways in which research on language universals and research on second language acquisition can benefit one another."[51] In each case, the editors provide a context from which Functional Specialization could give fresh efficient meanings to "pointing," "ways" and "benefits."

1. "research" – In *UHL* Greenberg remarks on "the heavy inertia that retards the development of adequate archive resources in linguistics. The need is urgent for reliable, detailed, comparable cross-linguistic data, accessible to researchers by topic."[52] The papers in Rutherford's volume "discuss a range of language phenomena…"[53] For example, on the topic of core grammar, reference is made in Rutherford's volume to the Zobl paper in which there is "phenomena that would be of interest to any researcher working with the UG [Universal Grammar] framework."[54]
2. "interpretation" – Data collecting would hand the baton to a group of interpreters that would yield grammars in the tentatively fullest sense of the word. From a functional standpoint, this group is free from the accumulation problem; it is focused on possible significance. Rutherford comments on "the interpretation of the word "universals"…[by] those engaged in work on grammatical theory…"[55] and the theoretical stance taken by both the Greenbergian and the Chomskyan approach to linguistic universals.[56] His volume also includes an article by Eckman that focuses on processes from which to discover "empirical significance…."[57]
3. "history" – Future historians would follow to give a more concrete Greenbergian account of grammars with their overlappings and variations of morphemes, marking, matings, tones, and typings. This would be is a plausible place for historical linguistics to lift into facticity the somewhat isolated grammars of individual languages. A full heuristics of the

functional specialty history would acknowledge that the grammatical plan of a language at a particular time is not the story of that grammar. Clearly, present studies in historical linguistics are a mere foreshadowing of the functional specialty History. Ultimately, the grammar of this or that language would be determined by specialists who would reach towards a dynamic ("synchronic") perspective.[58] The context of the Zobl paper cited by Rutherford anticipates the existence of "a larger framework of 'evolutive change' that has been well-attested historically."[59]

4. "dialectics" – History's impure factual accounting would become grist for the mill of an evaluative group, which assesses both the achievements, and the methods of achievement. In other words, this group would seek to evaluate, to produce their individual perspectives on achievements and grounds of achievements. They would thematize the basis of evaluation, of progress, and of an improvement of orientation. As it stands, contemporary investigations in linguistics labour under such truncated perspectives as "innate capacity" or "language instinct," etc. Moreover, the title of Hawkes' book *Explaining Language Universals*[60] pinpoints the fundamental orientation of this speciality. Yet in each case, there is no serious perspective on the real principles of language acquisition or language change. Nonetheless, recall Rutherford's earlier shadowy perspective that roughly identifies the contemporary struggle to achieve a basic "theoretical stance [amongst those who] would take the Greenbergian rather than the Chomskyan approach to language universals...[in a] consideration of language universals from several different perspectives....[T]his collection does indeed represent a diversity of perspectives on language universals and the ways in which they may illuminate...."[61]

5. "foundations" – The baton would be handed to a foundation group of specialists who would thematize the best perspective that each is capable of, of orientations and methodologies beneficial to the future of languages and linguistics, on the total heuristic dynamic of history. This specialty is very remotely hinted at by Rutherford's envisioning of

"orientation" and "methodology" for future linguistics that "will require positive evidence for mastery...[that] may go some way towards explaining..."[62] For example, in the Rutherford volumes, Kenji Hakuta entitles his article, "In what ways are language universals psychologically real?"[63] Moreover, Rutherford cites the "relationships in the context of the papers themselves [and] the ways in which the usefulness of these relationships as frameworks for interlanguage research might receive consistent articulation in terms of core grammar itself."[64] Furthermore, he points to the fact that "[t]he study of core grammar in theoretical linguistics is represented by a growing list of references [;] in particular Chomsky 1981a, 1981b and Koster (1978) [offer general characterization of core grammar.]"[65] Furthermore, "Bickerton's "bioprogram" also bears more than a passing resemblance to core grammar. And in his recent book we read that "in fact, bioprogram theory and Chomskyan formal universals fit rather well together...The bioprogram language would constitute a core structure for human language."[66]

6. "doctrines" – There are descriptive laws emergent from historical linguistics that can be identified, after the transforming efforts of dialectic and foundations, as linguistic policies or doctrines. Rutherford reports that the inquires by "Hirschbüler and Rivero (1981) further interpret the nature of core grammar to be a kind where a "rule of sentence grammar is an aggregate of dimensions: some belong to the core, and are unmarked; others belong to the periphery, and are marked....The application of L2 acquisition research of principles of universal grammar (UG) that derive from Extended Standard Theory (EST) and, in particular, core grammar is not unknown."[67] The Gass and Ard paper observes that "[t]he core-periphery principle might serve as another framework...."[68]

7. "systematics" – There is, further, the massive effort towards a full genetic systematics, which for some scholars, especially in the tradition of Greenberg, is the real goal of linguistics.[69] With reference to Givón's study, Rutherford remarks that "[i]n terms of core grammar then, one might consider the...possibility...a very possible relevance of core-periphery

phenomena to the kinds of discourse/syntax relationships discussed in Givón's paper as well as in earlier work of his.⁷⁰

8. "communications" – Systematics would mediate the particular selections and patterning that form the task of the final functional specialty, Linguistic Communications. A shadowy example of this specialty is contextualized in Rutherford, by "calling attention to...the reasons why insights revealed in these papers would interest a researcher.... It is obvious that the conference whose proceedings comprise this volume was convened in order that new light be shed on a research area of growing interest."⁷¹ "The best known research findings on language universals...include the insights offered by Greenberg (1963, 1966)....Many of the papers in this volume concern themselves – at some point, to varying degrees, explicitly or implicitly – [with research projects that] cite the work of Greenberg as well."⁷²

I have no doubt that the eightfold structure of global "academic"⁷³ collaboration, Functional Specialization, grounded by Generalized Empirical Method, would meet what I sense is the fundamental methodological challenge facing language studies. Moreover, I have noted that the required academic collaboration must be global. The evident grounds for this claim is that the fourth level tasks, specialties four and five, *dialectics* and *foundations*, are integral quests for the foundations of human progress.⁷⁴

---

[1] My use of the adjective "shadowy" here alludes to the limitations of common sense, first by the absence of GEM to ground the distinct but related tasks that are routinely but randomly tackled by scholars in the field. Secondly, there is the further problem of spontaneously viewing the tasks as a mere "filing system" that is organized under the headings of each specialty to be accessed by specialists. "Now in everyday, commonsense performance, all four levels are employed continuously without any explicit distinction between them. In that case no functional specialization arises, for what is sought is not the end of any particular level but the cumulative, composite resultant of the ends of all four levels. But in a scientific investigation the ends proper to particular levels may become the objective sought by operation on all four levels." Op. cit., *Method*, pp. 133-4.

[2] *The Americanist*. Oxford University Press, 2002. Online ISSN: 1468-4365.

[3] The movement towards standards is the issue governing the need for Generalized Empirical Method to replace the current literary tradition.
[4] *Essays in Criticism*. Oxford University Press, 2002. Online ISSN: 1471-6852.
[5] *The Cambridge Quarterly 2002*. Oxford University Press, 2002. Online ISSN: 1471-6836.
[6] *Forum for Modern Language Studies*. University of St Andrews, 2002. Online ISSN: 1471-6860.
[7] *Literary & Linguistic Computing 2002*. Oxford University Press, 2002. Online ISSN: 1477-4615.
[8] *Literature and Theology*. Oxford University Press, 2002. Online ISSN: 1477-4623.
[9] *Notes and Queries*. Oxford University Press, 2002. Online ISSN: 1471-6941.
[10] *The Review of English Studies*. Oxford University Press, 2002. Online ISSN: 1471-6968.
[11] *The Year's Work in English Studies*. The English Association, 2002. Online ISSN: 1471-6801.
[12] *Journal of Linguistics*. Cambridge University Press, 2002.
[13] It has become, for me, a routine exercise of adopting a methodological "eye" and "I" when reading articles, theses, books, etc., for discovering, invariably and inevitably, shadows of the specialties that *spontaneously* appear within various parts of *each*. Parts A and B provide a concrete illustration.
[14] I would note immediately that this analysis is *not* a critique of the content within each article; rather it confines itself to a strict *methodological focus* on the random appearance of the eight shadow specialties. A *full heuristics* would put each of the shadow specialties identified here into a new context. (This difficulty also lurks in the anticipations of Welleck, Warren, Greenberg, and Rutherford in the last section of this chapter). An understanding of the "new context" pivots on a grasp the term "functional." This is one of many of a complex meshing of unresolved issues relating to the absence of GEM, the absence of which renders the specialties in these articles merely "shadows." The reader is urged to view at once p. 250 of op. cit., *Method*, as well as op. cit., *The Subject*, pp. 8-12.
[15] *The Cambridge Quarterly*, Volume 30, Issue 2. Oxford University Press, June 2001.
[16] As a symbolic indicator, when each specialty is discussed in the work cited, a lower case letter distinguishes them as shadows of the specialties that spontaneously and randomly appear from future functional specialties (indicated by a capital letter) that would be grounded by generalized empirical method.
[17] With the need for internal checks on error and dishonesty there is the focus here on possible disorientations, biases and ideologies of historians, interpreters, researchers. The goal is a serious perspective on the real principles of advance in linguistics and literature. Again, the reader is invited to get a sense of the massive challenge with respect to "orientation" issued on p. 250 in op. cit., *Method*.

[18] *Dialectic* and *Foundations*, the fourth and fifth specializations require a full concrete attitude on the part of the specialists involved that asks, "What do you think you're doing?" The question of progress is a concrete question for the dialectician facing the past and the foundations specialist facing the future.
[19] Op. Cit., *The Cambridge Quarterly* 2002.
[20] To begin with, problems related to the first and eighth specialties, Research and Communications, are dominant. Unresolved issues with respect to the *selection*, *discovery* and *availability* of relevant data, written or otherwise, lurk within each study.
[21] Jean Gooder, "Henry James's Bostonians: The Voices of Democracy". *The Cambridge Quarterly*, Volume 30, Issue 2. Oxford University Press, June 2001, pp. 97-115.
[22] Ibid., "DeLillo's Libra and the Real," pp. 117-131.
[23] Ibid., "D. H. Lawrence as Verse Translator," pp. 133-150.
[24] Ibid., "Englands of the Mind," pp. 151-168.
[25] Ibid., p. 166.
[26] Ibid., p. 151.
[27] Ibid., pp. 166-7.
[28] Ibid., pp. 167-8.
[29] Ibid., pp. 151-2.
[30] Ibid., p. 167.
[31] Ibid., 152-3.
[32] Op. cit., *Theory of Literature*, p. 8.
[33] Ibid., pp. 57-69.
[34] Ibid., p. 142.
[35] Ibid., p. 158.
[36] Ibid., p. 186.
[37] Ibid., p. 252.
[38] I slide by the issue of the fundamental orientation of the doer of the task and its effect on the assessment of texts. Reflections on the nature of aesthetic meaning are also dodged here.
[39] Ibid., p. 238.
[40] Ibid., *Theory of Literature*, Chapters 8 to 11.
[41] Ibid., p. 81.
[42] Ibid., p. 94.
[43] Ibid., p. 110.
[44] Ibid., p. 125.
[45] Ibid., p. 226.
[46] Ibid., p. 139.
[47] Ibid., p. 139.
[48] Ibid., pp. 139-140.
[49] Greenberg's fundamental pointing is supplemented by references to shadows of the specialties identified in various parts of articles that appear in Rutherford, W. (ed.) *Language Universals and Second Language Acquisition* (LU). Philadelphia: John Benjamins Publishing Company, 1987.

50 Op. cit., *UHL*, Vol. 1, p. 2. Volume One deals with method and theory.
51 Op. cit., *LU*, p. 7. Quote is taken from page 11 of B. Comrie, "Why linguists need Language acquirers." *LU*, pp. 11-29.
52 Ibid. p. 26. The comment is made at the conclusion of Charles Ferguson's article in that volume, "Historical Background of Universals Research," pp. 8-28.
53 Ibid., p. 2.
54 Ibid., Helmut Zobl, "Uniformity and source-language variation across developmental continua." *LU*, pp. 219-222.
55 Ibid., p. 1.
56 Ibid.
57 Ibid., p. 8. F. Eckman, "Universals, typologies, and interlanguage." *LU*, pp. 79-105.
58 Op. cit., *UHL*, p. 64. See "Diachrony, Synchrony and Language Universals."
59 Op. cit., *LU*, p. 4.
60 Op. cit., *Explaining Language Universals*.
61 Op. cit., *LU*, pp. 1-2.
62 Ibid., p. 4.
63 Ibid., pp. 223-238. See Kenji Hakuta, "In what ways are language universals psychologically real?"
64 Ibid., p. 3.
65 Ibid.
66 Ibid., p. 5. See D. Bickerton, "The language bioprogram hypothesis and second language acquisition," pp. 141-160.
67 Ibid., p. 3.
68 Ibid., p. 4. See S. Gass, and J. Ard, "Second language acquisition and the ontology of language universals," pp. 33-68.
69 This is central to Greenberg's searching in op. cit., *UHL*, Vol. 1.
70 Op. cit., *LU*, pp. 4-5. See T. Givón, "Universals of discourse structure and second language acquisition," *LU*, pp. 109-136.
71 Op. cit., *LU*, p. 7.
72 Ibid., pp. 5-6.
73 Echoing note 38, op. cit. *BHT*, p. 104, "I write 'academic' here thus to recall the serious concerns of those in Academus' backyard. Such concerns stand in contrast with what is regularly meant now by the words 'merely academic' – which surely says something about contemporary learned discourse."
74 Recall the functional tasks of each: *Dialectic*: human wisdom looking to the past, coming up with a best story and the best basic directions, and *Foundations*: human wisdom looking to the future, expressing the best fundamental (in the sense that they are not tied to age, time, etc.) directions.

10
FUTURE POSSIBILITIES FOR THE HUMANITIES IN EDUCATION

The ultimate drive of this study has been directed toward a practical and progressive strategy for the Humanities, with its immense stake in language, as well as its urgent need for a structure of reflection and education with which to dissolve the culture of fragmentation. This inquiry has brought to light a philosophical strategy that, regrettably, has been neglected in linguistics, in literary studies, and in philosophies of language. The strategy is a precise phenomenology of human consciousness that, when pursued properly, involves a focal self-attention to simple personal experience in a manner that objectifies two core-attitudes: first, the experience of curiosity and wonder expressed as the dynamics of knowing ("What is it" → "Is it so?") and secondly, the experience of curiosity and wonder expressed as the dynamics of doing ("What is to be done?" → "Is it to be done?"). I presented empirical evidence with which to support the claim that these two core-attitudes are, in fact, the universals of human language. I have shown how language universals would ground a practical restructuring of language studies in a way that would shift critical reflection on linguistics and literature to a higher level, and ultimately, lift education in the Humanities out of a dominant cultural heritage that itself has been the very cause of this long-standing neglect.

The key to the proper pursuit of this strategy is to proceed on the basis of empirical observation. Such a procedure facilitates insight into the first principle of human language, and concomitantly, access to the existence and the meaning of language universals. And so, first, I quarried empirical data of language universals in the English language as it is rooted in an Indo-European tradition with parallel searches in Shakespeare, Beowulf, Donne, Joyce, Aristotle, Aquinas, The Bhagavad-Gita, and the experience of Helen Keller. Secondly, I quarried empirical data of language universals from parallel searches across cultures in dominant branches of the linguistic tree through Aryan, Semitic, African, Asian, Nordic, and Teutonic languages. Thirdly, in a dialectical analysis, I discussed how and why there is an absence of a parallel focus on language universals in a distinguished group of very influential writers. Fourthly, I related the meaning and significance of language universals to Lonergan's two-fold methodological strategy: Functional Specialization grounded by Generalized Empirical Method. I presented empirical evidence that supported and reinforced the acceptability and plausibility of this two-fold methodological strategy to language studies, and at the same time, indicated how a framework for critical reflection could possibly emerge through a detailed analysis that would invite Functional Specialization. This was done by an empirically focused, heuristic methodological analysis of, first, a spectrum of representative publications in language studies, secondly, a single representative journal in literary studies, and thirdly, the 'shadowy' anticipations of investigators representing literary and linguistic studies struggling toward, but falling far short of, a structure of reflection that would parallel the efficiency and progressiveness of Functional Specialization.

The underlying tone of this study has been one of long-term optimism. Its optimism is grounded further by the concrete discovery of another fundamental principle of human language: in each human, from the infant to the elder, language emerges in "a cumulative series of shifts from babbling to talk."[1] This potential of human drive from babbling to talk resonates powerfully in this passage by Alfred, Lord Tennyson:

> Behold, we know not anything;
> -----
> ...what am I?
> An infant crying in the night:
> An infant crying for the light:
> And with no language but a cry.[2]

Focused empirical observation exposes the core structure of language universals that, with proper attention, reveals the richness of Vedic desire, a luminous expression of the integrated human. For the human empirical cry "in the night," is the expression of incarnate core desire in the whole human, of the integral heuristic structure of quest stretching forth with the probing: "what am I?" Tennyson's symbolic expression of human performance presents an epiphany of empirical data from which to lift toward adequate linguistic feedback[3] on researching, teaching, and ultimately, shifting critical reflection on linguistics and literature to a level of talk about human beings as they actually are. Talk begins with the data of quest, which is questing 'senseAbility,' accessible by attending to a simple personal experience – a point made clearly in Aristotle's famous observation about wonder being a beginning, and by Aquinas' famous admonition: "We can all experience in ourselves...."[4] Orientation toward the initial epiphany of the shift from babbling to talk, then, is a matter of undertaking the empirical process of "meeting yourself."

Optimism must remain long term. Our integral Vedic reaching has been fragmented in a way that has compromised human expression with a globally impoverished babble of "no language but a cry."[5] In spite of the discovery of the existence and meaning of language universals that would liberate us from 'babbling' extra-scientific opinion, the Humanities will continue to be frustrated by this 'noise,' with its present orientation, shaping 'normal' student and teacher background, by "educating them out of their minds."[6] With language solidly colonized by conceptualist thinking and expression in present-day academic life, truncated subjectivity and commonsense eclecticism rule the day. And so, sadly, education at all levels will for the foreseeable future continue to rue the day, trapped in a stagnant state of "no language but a cry," rendering the conditions for a new pragmatism in education extremely remote.

How are these conditions manifested? Halfway through the Twentieth Century Lonergan observed of the scene in education that "the fundamental problem is the horizon of the educationalist – of the person or group that has the power and the money, that runs the bureaucracy, that makes the decisions – and the horizon of the teacher. Insofar as their horizons are insufficiently enlarged, there will be difficulties all along the line."[7] Underpinning that confinement of horizon is the fact that "[t]he neglected subject does not know himself. The truncated subject not only does not know himself but also is unaware of his ignorance and so, in one way or another, concludes that what he does not know does not exist."[8] Clearly, these appalling conditions desperately cry out for a critical horizon grounded by Generalized Empirical Method, with which to enlarge the horizon of "the educationalist" sufficiently to shift the culture of pragmatism to a luminous new meaning for human institutions,[9] from the present cultural abomination that binds the purpose and goal of education to centralized global economic ideology,[10] and its preservation by a dominant bureaucratic hierarchy.[11] This demoralizing of human practicality neither acknowledges the limitations of common sense, nor grasps the fact that "Theoretic understanding...seeks to solve problems.... Still common sense is concerned not with remote but with proximate possibilities."[12] Its fixation on the proximate, the palpable, devotedly clings to commonsense eclecticism for its method. And so while theoretic understanding[13]

> has come to dominate the field of physical research, its implications made no great impression elsewhere....[I]t does not seem to have brought about a startling revolution in economics, or sociology, or political theory, or psychology, or psychiatry, or educational theory, or pedagogy, or genetics....[This] is regrettable. For the whole orientation of the human sciences would be changed, if...the science of [humankind would be] concerned principally with...intelligence [viz. theoretic understanding]...it [would then] be applied through...intelligence....[14]

Thus, in classroom routines "all along the line," Aquinas' comment remains terribly true, "inform students of a bundle of opinions and they depart empty-headedly."[15]

The implementation of Generalized Empirical Method would radically transform the pragmatics of education.[16] Its practice would enlarge the horizon of the educationalist sufficiently with which to acknowledge a differentiation of consciousness that would place theoretic understanding[17] at the center of education. The teacher and the student, then, would become language detectives, poised in potency, engaged in isomorphic performance that, through a cumulative series of shifts from babbling to talk, would reveal the core of their being. The interplay is captured in a simple slogan: when teaching children language, one is teaching children children.[18] Concomitantly, when teaching children language, one is teaching the teacher the teacher. Put another way, a teacher engaged in the process of "discovering oneself in oneself" would be poised to mediate the journey in which students would "discover themselves in themselves." While proceeding with a dual focus:

> [t]he teacher can help and stimulate and guide...the formulation of what is grasped by the act of understanding. But it is the pupil himself becoming habituated to an intellectual pattern of experience that is at once the fundamental condition of the whole process of teaching and at the same time its great fruit. Insofar as you are teaching people geometry, for example, you are using an implement that is magnificently adapted to habituating people to the intellectual pattern of experience. Even though they never bother their heads about geometry for the rest of their lives, at least they have lived at certain moments of their lives in the intellectual pattern of experience. They have some familiarity with the way things go on there, and they have a greater facility of doing that sort of thing on other occasions. Moreover, from the fact that they have been through the experience, there results a shift in the center of gravity in their experiencing. That shift in the center of gravity, that habituation to a differentiated consciousness, is a fruit of education, but an indirect fruit. It is only by doing particular subjects that that fruit results.[19]

Its fruit, for education and the Humanities, would be the objectification of human understanding "all along the line" of inquiry, a method with which to "habituate people to the intellectual pattern of experience," thereby promoting "a greater facility of doing that sort of thing when doing particular subjects" such as language and literature.

We turn our focus from the lag associated with the absence of theoretic understanding, to a concurrent lag associated with the historical shift from a classicist to an empirical notion of culture,[20] in fragmented academic routines that are beginning to cry out for a new creative approach that would invite Functional Specialization. Thus, the shift to an empirical notion of culture brings with it the urgency for a "framework for collaborative creativity,"[21] a need Lonergan makes clear in the context of theology:

> When the classicist notion of culture prevails, theology is conceived as a permanent achievement, and then one discourses on its nature. When culture is conceived empirically, theology is known to be an ongoing process, and then one writes on its method. A contemporary method would conceive those tasks, in the context of modern science, modern scholarship, modern philosophy, of historicity, collective practicality and coresponsibility.[22]

The need extends to the human cry for a fresh, global perspective on the contemporary meaning of "science," "method," and "methodology" to thematize an adequate investigative structure, a genetic division of labour relevant not only to language studies, but to any cultural endeavour, in the quest to cycle tasks of discernment in the field of language studies, in an effort to continue to discover as best we can how language works and how we should roll with it. Such a perspective would acknowledge that a further pragmatic principle has been forced upon us by the specializations and fragmentations and discoveries of these past centuries. Indeed, the need for a division of labour is suggested, not by some arbitrarily imposed group of tasks, but de facto by the fermentation of centuries, even in post-modern expressions that would scorn categories and canons.

Amidst all this short-term gloom, it must be asked, what then is the probability of future economists, politicians, scientists, doctors, lawyers, teachers, clergy, etc., undergoing, in their formative years as students, "a [horizon] shift in the center of gravity in their experiencing," with which to be habituated to theoretical understanding, to respond wisely and responsibly to the human cry for fresh global perspective? Similarly, what is the probability of a budding generation of scholars in linguistics and literary study undergoing "a [horizon] shift in the center of gravity in its experiencing," to be habituated to theoretical understanding, to respond wisely and responsibly to the human cry for fresh global perspective? Furthermore, what is the probability that the current academic culture will summon sufficient horizon to commit to the legitimacy of, and need for, Generalized Empirical Method and Functional Specialization in any field or line of inquiry with which to seriously cultivate and sustain human dignity, efficiency, and progress on a global scale? These questions, too, invite short-term gloom. For "the monster that has stood forth in our day,"[23] has given birth to a crippling paradox that, in the name of reason and progress, systematically and cumulatively prolongs chronic human problems while contributing to social and cultural decline.[24] Certainly, then, no one could be blamed for being pessimistic in the short term, or for being inclined to estimate that the level of probability of academic growth would be less than one percent.[25]

Is there any room for optimism with which to anticipate a slight but significant shift in the respect for human senseAbility?[26] Could it be seeded here and there, in this classroom and that, by pedagogic attempts at Generalized Empirical Method and Functional Specialization,[27] taking a stand against the conceptualist pseudo-rationalism and pseudo-pragmatism that possesses our schools and departments of education and fragments academic efforts? In the context of a new philosophy of language and a new grammatology, Jackendoff offers this advice:

> In my opinion, if one wishes to join the conversation about the nature of language, one must recognize and acknowledge [its] complexity. One need not have an account of all of it, but one may not willfully ignore it and still expect to be allowed in the game. This is the minimum that scientific responsibility demands.[28]

Might I suggest that this study has met Jackendoff's admonition to the extent that it has lifted "the conversation about the nature of language" study into a context that the Greenberg School, reaching quite beyond previous efforts such as that of Chomsky, was looking for and grasping at? The context has emerged in this study as a sort of 'half-way house', in the form of a two-pronged strategy to cut down the elements of restructuring to its two key components: the focal shift in grammatology and the functional relating of sub-fields of linguistics.

What is this focal shift leading toward?[29] The full reach of the line of inquiry we call the philosophy of language, adequately expressed and expanded, will seek to penetrate the entire scope of grammar studies both in the re-cataloguing of linguistic families and in the redefining of the standard parts of speech. The full reach will freshen up the question, "what is metaphysics?" by focusing, in Lonergan's terms, on the isomorphism of question and questioner: for he has remarked no less that "metaphysics rests on the major premise of the isomorphism of the structures of knowing and of proportionate being..."[30] Lonergan, envisioning the full reach, was neither 'out there' nor 'in here' but in being,[31] 'some how' focused on a quite new metaphysics of words and of grammar, on the structured concrete "what" and "is" that is all humans in history. In Chapter 17 of *Insight*, Lonergan puts the challenge into context for a metaphysics of words and of grammar: "A scientific interpretation is concerned to formulate the relevant insights and judgments, and to do so in a manner that is consonant with scientific collaboration and scientific control."[32] As such, Functional Specialization, Lonergan's great achievement, gives structure to the Hegelian insight:

> As the labor of introspection proceeds, one stumbles upon Hegel's insight that the full objectification of the human spirit is the history of the human race. It is in the sum of the products of common sense and common nonsense, of the sciences and the philosophies, of moralities and religions, of social orders and cultural achievements, that there is mediated, set before us the mirror in which we can behold, the originating principle of human aspiration and human attainment and failure. Still, if that vast panorama is to be explored methodically, there is the

prior need of method"[33]

His reflection on Hegel envisages the dialectical reach of the whole of humanity in its minding, from which to shape its future minding. His focus on the question about question in the concrete takes in all occurrences of questers and questions and furnishes the fundamental underpinning for a fresh, global perspective on the meaning of "science," "method," and "methodology." Over the long haul, then, the task of working toward elevating language to an explanatory perspective is to continue to fantasize foundationally, as did Lonergan, toward a perspective on a fuller explanatory heuristic of words.[34] "It takes as its starting point and clue the discovery of some precise issue on which undoubtedly one was mistaken,"[35] the issue for us being the massive historical confusion of viewpoints on meaning, the proximate versions of which dominate reflection on language, the alienating grammatical structures of Panini, the mediaevals and the moderns in their talk of words as parts of speech. I suspect that a plan that seeks to rise to the level of a scientific determination of classes would move towards strategic description meshed with crucial experimenting from which to arrive at the beginning of explanation.[36]

A preliminary, then, would involve the employment of a simple empirical procedure with which to discover "The keys to. Given! A way a lone...a long the...."[37] And so in a Joycean round, we are back to the beginning of this chapter as well as this study.

I conclude by expressing hope that my labour will be viewed as an invitation to those who are at present struggling with the problem of language universals and to those who are trying to find some principle of integration in the entire field; for it is a field that, thus far, has succeeded in dodging scientific thinking. As such, I believe I have presented a modest beginning in response to Jackendoff's exigent call for "scientific responsibility," with the twist that the onset of scientific responsibility must be seeded by human senseAbility if it would transform language study, and ultimately, pragmatism in education. The groan of history resonates with human senseAbility's empirical cry in the night, a core human drive that can no longer be ignored or abused if education in the Humanities is to meet the minimum that scientific responsibility demands, with which to be allowed in the "game of the name." Indeed, no line of human inquiry can go on without inviting, if not sharing, in a legitimate venture into theoretic worlds. Without it one lives in the illusion of knowledge.

Finally, I do not expect that the boldness of asking what precisely is going on in language studies, or urging the implementation of Generalized Empirical Method and Functional Specialization, will be embraced with a surge, much less with a sudden burst. Nevertheless, I anticipate that over time this focal shift will ultimately win the day; for I am not only hopeful, I am convinced that time and necessity is on the side of this relevant and inevitable shift of culture that would not only jettison critical reflection on linguistics and literature to a new level, but also ultimately lift education in the Humanities toward richer research and more adequate communication. And so, in the spirit of long-term optimism

> I can but trust that good shall fall
> At last – far off – at last, to all,
> And every winter change to spring.
> So runs my dream...[38]

---

[1] Op. cit., *BHT*, p. 16.
[2] Alfred (Lord) Tennyson, "In Memoriam A.H.H.," Canto 54, op. cit, *Norton*, p. 1058.
[3] Op. cit., *Method*, p. 48, 88 and p. 97. Op. cit., *ICT*, pp. 90-95.
[4] Op. cit., *Summa Theologiae*, 1, q. 84, a. 7 c.
[5] Op. cit, *Norton*, p. 1058.
[6] Op. cit., *BHT*, p. 28.
[7] Op. cit., *Topics in Education (CWL 10)*, p. 106.
[8] Op. cit., *The Subject*, p. 8.
[9] See op. cit., *ICT*, Chapter 31, "Conversatons," pp. 119-124. That chapter brings Lonergan's diagram on p. 48 of op. cit., *Method*, into focus as the luminous basis for a structure of the human good. Also, see *Insight*, Chapter XVIII, "The Possibility of Ethics." In the context of language study, see *ICT*, Chapter 24, "An International Ethic," pp. 90-95.
[10] Clearly, global economic and bureaucratic practice and its stranglehold on human process opens up a large and complex topic well beyond the scope of this book. While I cannot enlarge on it any further, the reader may wish to follow up first with op. cit., *Method*, p. 357: "The basic form of ideology is the

self-justification of alienated man." The pervasiveness of this false pragmatism threatens the very survival of human dignity and freedom. Lonergan discusses this brand of alienation in *For A New Political Economy (CWL 21)*, University of Toronto Press, 1998, Part 1, Section 9. His appeal for the preservation of human dignity in global economic practice reveals, first, how tightly its world and its fate is tied to the world of education, and secondly, the shift of horizon that would invite its reversal: "And for society to progress towards that or any other goal it must fulfill one condition. It cannot be a titanothere, a beast with a three-ton body and a ten-ounce brain. It must not direct its main effort to the ordinary final product of standard of living but to the overhead product of cultural implements. It must not glory in its widening, in adding industry to industry, and feeding the soul of man with an abundant demand for labor. It must glory in its deepening, in the pure deepening that adds aggregate leisure, to liberate many entirely and all increasingly to the field of cultural activities. It must not boast of science on the ground that science fills its belly. It must not glue its nose to the single track of this or that department. It must lift its eyes more and more to the more general and the more difficult fields of speculation, for it is from them that it has to derive the delicate compound of unity and freedom in which alone progress can be born, struggle, and win through."

[11] Lonergan condemns bureaucratic practice in "Respect for Human Dignity," *The Canadian Messenger of the Sacred Heart*, July 1953. Elsewhere, Lonergan's critical view of bureaucracy makes transparent the insidious mechanism of stagnation that is devoted to conserving and insulating the dominance of a centralized global economic ideology and its enslavement of educational practice: "Such a state of affairs interferes with creativity. It is not enough just to have a new idea, even if the idea is just what is wanted. The idea has to combine with power, with wealth, with popular notions, before it can be realized. It cannot simply emerge from the man on the spot, diffuse, give rise to new potentialities in a chain reaction. Developments become lopsided, curtailed. Completion of the development is demanded by disaffection, but it cannot emerge in the normal fashion of the spread of an idea. It has to come by management, from above downward, not from below upward. Management always needs more power. Without a constant increase in power, management is not able to control all the outside factors that might interfere with its plans. If it cannot exclude those factors, it cannot achieve its results. And so there occurs the rise and growth of bureaucratic hierarchy. In spontaneous developments, the new ideas come where they may to the man on the spot who is intelligent, sees the possibilities, and goes ahead at his own risk. But in the bureaucracy the intelligent man ceases to be the initiator. He does not have the power, the connections, the influence, to put his ideas into practice. He becomes a consultant, an expert, called in by the bureaucracy. Activity is slowed down to the pace of routine paper work. Style and form, that are inevitable when the man who has the idea is running things, yield to standardization and uniformity. Wisdom and faith yield to eclecticism and

syncretism: Pick the best ideas, and the ideas will suit everybody. The process of mimesis, of the people who were carried on in the movement even though they did not quite understand it, changes into drudgery and routine, with no understanding of what is going on. They keep on doing it because they have to live. Creativity has fewer and fewer opportunities for significant achievement. The lone individual is more and more driven onto the margin of the big process, of what is really going on. The masses demand security, distraction, entertainment, pleasure, and they have a decreasing sense of shame." Op. cit., *Topics in Education*, pp. 60-61.

[12] Op. cit., *Insight*, p. 417 [442].

[13] I take this opportunity to cite Butterfield's comment that the emergence of theoretical understanding "outshines everything since the rise of Christianity and reduces the Renaissance and Reformation to the rank of mere episodes, mere internal displacements...." Op. cit., *The Rise of Modern Science*, p. vii.

[14] Op. cit., "Respect for Human Dignity," p. 2.

[15] Op. cit., Quodl., IV, a. 18. "*Nihil scientiae vel intellectus acquiret, sed vacuus adscedet.*"

[16] Fundamentally, it would liberate educational schemes from the present "cultural *ethos* of serial killing: [Philip McShane notes,] "Jack and Jill the rippers are not, then, the oddities: the oddities are those few teachers who can somehow beat the system, the unsung heroines and heroes. But Jack and Jill in the classrooms are really only victims: the knife in their hand is wielded by the cult that generates the texts and the courses, that seeks to control the formation of teachers in committedly truncated B.Ed. programs. I am writing of a dedicated truncation, blood-spilling, of the next generation, at school and university level in almost all topics." Philip McShane, "How Might I Become a Better Teacher?" Of this article (currently unpublished) McShane comments: "I have already written on this topic...under the title "A Reform of Classroom Performance..." The article is in *Divyadaan* (13), 2002, pp. 279-309. A following article is also on the topic: "The Wonder of Water: The Legacy of Lonergan," *Divyadaan* (15), 2004, pp. 457-475.

[17] Lonergan introduces theoretic understanding as the "intellectual pattern of experience." See op. cit., *Insight*, "Patterns of Experience," pp. 181-9 [204-12].

[18] Once again, I am indebted to Philip McShane who first coined the slogan. Originally he said: "The interplay of philosophy and world is then captured in my simple slogan, *when teaching children geometry, one is teaching children children,* where *geometry* can be replaced by any other topic, and *children* replaced by any age group." This is a pedagogical strategy that also includes the person who is teaching.

[19] Op. cit., *Topics in Education*, p. 116.

[20] Hence, there will be considerable resistance to my position that the "proper pursuit" of a phenomenology of human consciousness is to proceed on the basis of empirical observation.

[21] Op. cit., *Method*, p. xi.

[22] Ibid.

[23] Op. cit., *Method*, p. 40. This monster may thus be cast as the truncated subject, the general bias of which must be overcome by the hero of a type described by Jung: "If a man is a hero, he is a hero because in the first reckoning, he did not let the monster devour him, but subdued it not once but many times," C.G. Jung, "The relations between the Ego and the Unconscious," *Collected Works*, Vol. 7, Princeton University Press, p.173.

[24] See op. cit., *Insight*, "The Longer Cycle of Decline," p. 226 [251].

[25] A. Maslow, *Towards a Psychology of Being*. Princeton: Van Nostrand, 1968, p. 204. Maslow speaks of less than one percent of adults growing.

[26] Philip McShane identifies the context for the beginner out of which could emerge the basis for long-term optimism in op. cit., *BHT*, p. 140: "What I try to share here certainly could be of some inspiration to a beginner in self-discovery, for unless you have been drifting mindlessly into your twenties and beyond, you resonate someway with what I consider the root-stimulus of adequate living, expressed in two short passages of Lonergan's *Insight*, conventionally readable with any venture into philosophy, good or bad: 'Against the objectivity that is based on intelligent inquiry and critical reflection…there stands the native bewilderment of the existential subject, revolted by mere animality, unsure of his way through the maze of philosophies, trying to live without a known purpose, suffering despite an unmotivated will, threatened with inevitable death and, before death, with disease and even insanity.' *Insight*, p. 385. [*CWL* 3, p. 410] 'The concrete being of man, then, is being in process. His existing lies in developing. His unrestricted desire to know heads him ever towards a known unknown. His sensitivity matches the operator of his intellectual advance with a capacity and a need to respond to a further reality than meets the eye and to grope his way towards it. Still, this basic, indeterminately directed dynamism has its ground in potency; it is without the settled assurance and efficacy of form; it tends to be shouldered out of the busy day, to make its force felt in the tranquility of darkness, in the solitude of loneliness, in the shattering upheavals of personal or social disaster. *Insight*, p. 625. [*CWL* 3, p. 648]'"

[27] See op. cit., *ICT*, Chapter 32, "Putting our Global Minding in Order," pp. 124-128.

[28] Op. cit., *The Foundations of Language*, p. 18.

[29] The future direction of this study is discussed in some detail in Part 3 of op. cit., "Lonergan and the Meaning of Word."

[30] Op. cit., *Insight*, p. 576 [599].

[31] This relates to the philosophical position, "extreme realism," or in Lonergan's terms, "intellectual conversion." This issue is fundamental, lengthy and complex and I raise it in the context of language study in the article "Lonergan and the Meaning of Word," op. cit. While I have not touched upon this issue in this study, it is no less a crucial factor in fostering empirical evidence with which to support the plausibility and credibility of my thesis. Should the reader venture to explore this zone, I would note that helpful for me over many years of reflection, is the analogy of the Mobius-strip to the

extent that a Mobius-strip theory of consciousness one-sidedly excludes any two-sidedness in the appreciation of the meaning of the word "is." The anomaly of confrontational two-sidedness is the central warp in both logic and phenomenology.

[32] Op. cit., *Insight*, p. 586 [608]. The context of this statement is Section 3.8 "Some Canons for a Methodical Hermeneutics."

[33] I quote from p. 14 of a Lonergan archival file labeled A697. It contains a typescript numbered pp. 8-23.

[34] In the new functional specialist context, postmodern philosophy is to be identified with the activities of the fourth and fifth specialties. In the other specialties there is certainly "the use of the categories," but the nature and genesis of the categories is the focus of these two specialties.

[35] Op. cit., *Insight*, p. 714 [736].

[36] Here I recall Lonergan in op. cit., *Insight*, p. 464 [489], in a way that includes the necessary twist toward the questioner: "[Self-]study of [language] begins from the thing-for-us, from the [linguistic data] as exhibited to our senses. A first step is a descriptive differentiation of different parts..." The long haul, of course, is to discover the metaphysical equivalents of the eight parts of speech. In ibid., *Insight*, p. 503 [526], Lonergan observes, "Since metaphysical analysis has a quite different basis from grammatical or logical analysis, one must not expect any one-to-one correspondence between metaphysical elements and grammatical or logical elements."

[37] James Joyce, *Finnegan's Wake*. New York: Penguin Books, p. 628. Appropriately, then, we end with a puzzle for the reader, the clue of which includes Joyce's deliberate omitting of the full stop at the end of the novel. I am thus quoting from the last sentence at the end of *Finnegan's Wake*. The sentence then continues at the beginning of the novel with "riverrun, past Eve and Adam's...."

[38] Op. cit., "In Memorium A.H.H.," *Norton*, p. 1058.

SELECTED BIBLIOGRAPHY

Ahrenberg, L., *Interrogative Structures of Swedish*, Uppsala University, 1987.
Ali, Dr. S., *Arabic for Beginners*, New York: Hippocrene Books, 1994.
Americanist, The, Oxford University Press, 2002, Online ISSN: 1468-4365.
Aquinas, St. Thomas. *Summa Theologiae*, Christian Classics Inc.
Aristotle, *The Basic Works of Aristotle*, McKeon, R. (ed.). New York: Random House, 1941.
———. *Introduction to Aristotle*. McKeon, R. (ed.). New York: The Modern Library, 1947.
Benton, J., "Lonergan and the Meaning of Word," *Journal of Macrodynamic Analysis*, (4) 2004.
Benton, J., Drage, A., McShane, P., *Introducing Critical Thinking*, Halifax: Axial Publishing, 2005.
Beowulf, The Norton Anthology of English Literature, The, Vol. 1, New York: W.W. Norton, 1974.
Bhagavad-Gita, The, Sargeant, W. (trans.), State University of New York Press, 1984.
Bhagavad-Gita, The, Stoler Millar, B. (trans.), New York: Bantam Books, 1986.
Booth, S., *Shakespeare's Sonnets*, Yale University Press, 1977.
Butterfield, H., *The Origin of Modern Science*, Toronto: Clarke, Irwin & Co., 1968.
Byrne, P. H., *Analysis and Science in Aristotle*, State University of New York Press, 1997.
"Caedmon's Hymn," *The Norton Anthology of English Literature, The*, Vol. 1, New York: W.W. Norton, 1974.
Cambridge Quarterly, The. Oxford University Press, 2002, Online ISSN: 1471-6836.
———. Volume 30, Issue 2. Oxford University Press, June 2001.
Cantarino, V., *Modern Arabic Prose*, Indiana University Press, 1974.
Chomsky, N., *Reflections on Language*, New York: Pantheon Books, 1975.
Collinson, W.E., *The German Language Today. Its Patterns and Background*, London: Hutchinson University, 1968.

Selected Bibliography (cont'd)

Comrie, B., *Language Universals and Linguistic Typology*, Oxford: Blackwell, 1992.
Coulson, M., *Sanskrit*, London: Hodder & Stoughton, 1992.
Cram, D., and Pollnitz, C., "D. H. Lawrence as Verse Translator," *The Cambridge Quarterly*, Volume 30, Issue 2, Oxford University Press, June 2001.
De Man, P., *Blindness and Insight*, Oxford University Press, 1971.
Derrida, J., *Of Grammatology*, Spivak, G.C. (trans.) Johns Hopkins University Press, 1998.
Donne, J., "The Ecstacy," *The Norton Anthology of English Literature, The*, Vol. 1, New York: W.W. Norton, 1974.
_____. "Song," *The Norton Anthology of English Literature, The*, Vol. 1, New York: W.W. Norton, 1974.
Drage, A., *Thinking Woman*, Cape Breton: Axial Publishing, 2006.
Essays in Criticism, Oxford University Press, 2002, Online ISSN: 1471-6852.
Eckhard-Black, C., Whittle, R., *Cassell's Contemporary German*, New York: Simon and Schuster, 1992.
Ellmann, R., *James Joyce*, Oxford University Press, 1981.
Fodor, J., *Linguistics: The Cambridge Survey*, Vol. III, (ed.) F.J. Newmeyer, Cambridge University Press, 1988.
Forum for Modern Language Studies, University of St Andrews, 2002, Online ISSN: 1471-6860.
Freeman, N., *Shakespeare's First Texts*, Vancouver: Folio Scripts, 1994.
Gervais, D., "Englands of the Mind," *The Cambridge Quarterly*, Volume 30, Issue 2, Oxford University Press, June 2001.
Gooder, J., "Henry James's Bostonians: The Voices of Democracy," *The Cambridge Quarterly*, Volume 30, Issue 2, Oxford University Press, June 2001.
Greenberg, J. H., *Universals of Human Language* (Vols. I-IV), Stanford University Press, 1978.
Hawkes, J.A., *Explaining Language Universals*, Oxford: Blackwells, 1988.
Hindustani in Three Months, New Delhi: Vikas Publishing House, 1993.

Selected Bibliography (cont'd)

Hutchinson, S., "DeLillo's Libra and the Real," *The Cambridge Quarterly*, Volume 30, Issue 2, Oxford University Press, June 2001.
Jackendoff, R., *Foundations of Language*, Oxford University Press, 2002.
Journal of Linguistics, Cambridge University Press, 2002.
Joyce, J., *Ulysses*, London: Penguin Books, 1986.
———. *Finnegan's Wake*, New York: Penguin Books, 1967.
Jung, C.G., *Collected Works*, Vol.7, Princeton University Press.
Kavanagh, P., *The Complete Poems of Patrick Kavanagh*, New York: Hand Press, 1972.
Keifer, F. (ed.), *Questions and Answers*, Dordrecht: D. Reidel, 1983.
Keller, H., *The Story of My Life*, New York: Doubleday, 1955.
———. *The World I Live In*, The New York Review of Books, 2003.
Kibberd, D., *Inventing Ireland. The Literature of the Modern Nation*, Harvard University Press, 1993.
Lash, J. P., *Helen and Teacher*, New York: Delacorte Press, 1980.
Lederer, H., *Reference Grammar of the German Language*, New York: Charles Scribner's Sons, 1969.
Literary & Linguistic Computing 2002, Oxford University Press, 2002, Online ISSN: 1477-4615.
Literature and Theology, Oxford University Press, 2002, Online ISSN: 1477-4623.
Lonergan, B., "Christology Today," *A Third Collection: Papers by Bernard J. F. Lonergan, S.J.*, Paulist Press, 1985.
———. "Cognitional Structure," *Introducing the Thought of Bernard Lonergan*, Philip McShane (ed.), London: Darton, Longman & Todd, 1973.
———. *Insight: A Study of Human Understanding*, 1958, 1992, Toronto: University of Toronto Press, 1992.
———. *For A New Political Economy*, University of Toronto Press, 1998.
———. *Method in Theology*, New York: Herder and Herder, 1972.
———. *Phenomenology and Logic*, Toronto: University of Toronto Press, 2001.

Selected Bibliography (cont'd)

_____. "Respect for Human Dignity," *The Canadian Messenger of the Sacred Heart*, July 1953.
_____. *Subject, The*, Milwaukee: Marquette University Press, 1968.
_____. "The Form of Inference," *Collection, Collected Works*, Vol. 4, University of Toronto Press, 1988.
_____. *Topics in Education*, Toronto: University of Toronto Press, 1993.
_____. *Verbum: Word and Idea in Aquinas*, Toronto: University of Toronto Press, 1997.
Loogman, A., *Swahili Grammar and Syntax*, Duquesne University Press, 1965.
Maslow, A., *Towards a Psychology of Being*, Princeton: Van Nostrand, 1968.
McShane, P., *Brief History of Tongue, A*, Halifax: Axial Press, 1998.
_____. "Cantower XIX," www.philipmcshane.ca, October 2003.
_____. *Redress of Poise, The: The End of Lonergan's Work*, www.philipmcshane.ca
_____. *Shaping of the Foundations*, University Press of America, 1976.
_____. *Wealth of Self and Wealth of Nations*, www.philipmcshane.ca.
Newmeyer, F.J. (ed.), *Linguistics: The Cambridge Survey*, Vol. III, Cambridge University Press, 1988.
Notes and Queries, Oxford University Press, 2002. Online ISSN: 1471-6941.
Pert, C., *Molecules and Emotion*, New York: Touchstone, 1997.
Pinker, S., *The Language Instinct*, New York: William Morrow & Co., 1994.
Po-fei Huang, P., *Cantonese Dictionary*, Yale University Press, 1970.
Plato, *Meno*, Sharples, R. W. (ed.), Wiltshire: Aris and Phillips Ltd., 1985.
Review of English Studies, The, Oxford University Press, 2002, Online ISSN: 1471-6968.
Rutherford, W. (ed.), *Language Universals and Second Language Acquisition*, Philadelphia: John Benjamins Publishing Company, 1987.

Selected Bibliography (cont'd)

Shakespeare, W., *The Complete Works*, Harrison, G.B. (ed.). New York: Harcourt, Brace, 1968.

———. *The First Folio of Shakespeare 1623*, New York: Applause Books, 1995.

———. *The Tragedie of Macbeth*, New York: Applause Books, 1998.

———. *The Tragedie of Hamlet*, New York: Applause Books, 2000.

Standard English-Swahili Dictionary, The, Oxford University Press, 1953.

Synge, J.L., *Science, Sense and Nonsense*, London: Cape, 1951.

Tennyson, A. (Lord), "In Memoriam A.H.H.," Canto 54, *The Norton Anthology of English Literature*, Vol. 2, New York: W.W. Norton, 1974.

"Wanderer, The," *The Norton Anthology of English Literature, The*, Vol. 1, New York: W.W. Norton, 1974.

Webb, V. and Kembo-Sure, *African Voices*, Oxford University Press, 2000.

Wellek, R. and Warren, A., *Theory of Literature*, New York: Harcourt, Brace and World, 1956.

Welmers, W. E., *African Language Structures*, University of California Press, 1973.

Wilson, P. M., *Simplified Swahili*, Nairobi: Longman Kenya Ltd., 1977.

Wordsworth, W., "Ode: Intimations of Immortality From Recollections of Early Childhood," *The Norton Anthology of English Literature*, Vol. 2, New York: W.W. Norton, 1974.

Year's Work in English Studies, The, The English Association, 2002, Online ISSN: 1471-6801.

Appendix A

This section presents further empirical data of the dynamics of knowing and the dynamics of doing from a sampling of languages of the world.* In the likelihood of an absence of idiomatic subtlety in the selection of data in these samples, we gratefully invite further correction and refinement by experts, who are fluent in the languages presented, either in this book, or in future publications in which this species of linguistic data is presented.

List of data to follow:

1. French
2. Egyptian
3. Cantonese
4. Hindi
5. Mandarin
6. Polish
7. Portuguese
8. Punjabi
9. Russian
10. Spanish
11. Thai
12. Urdu
13. Welsh

---

* I wish to thank my grade twelve philosophy students at West Hill Secondary School in Owen Sound, Ontario, Canada, for generating data of samples numbered 2 to 13.

1) French

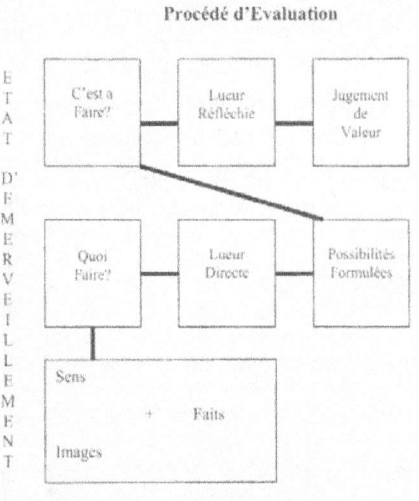

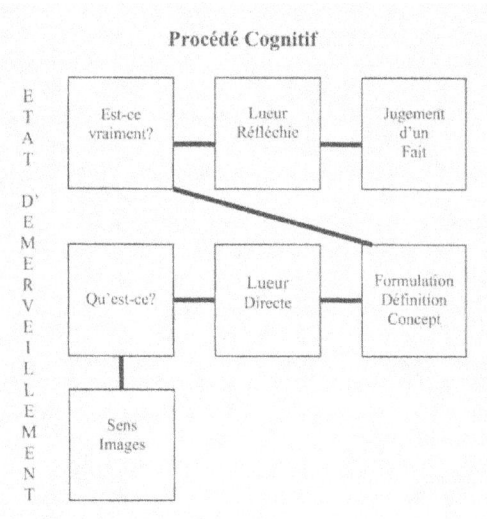

2) Egyptian

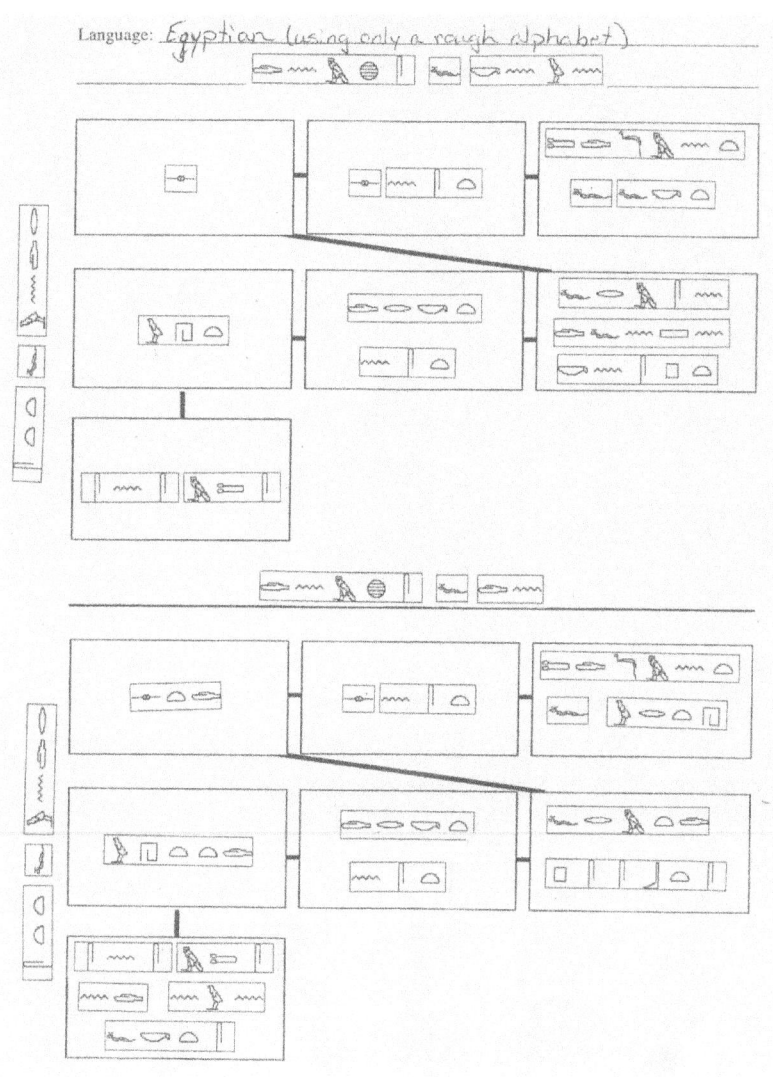

3) Cantonese

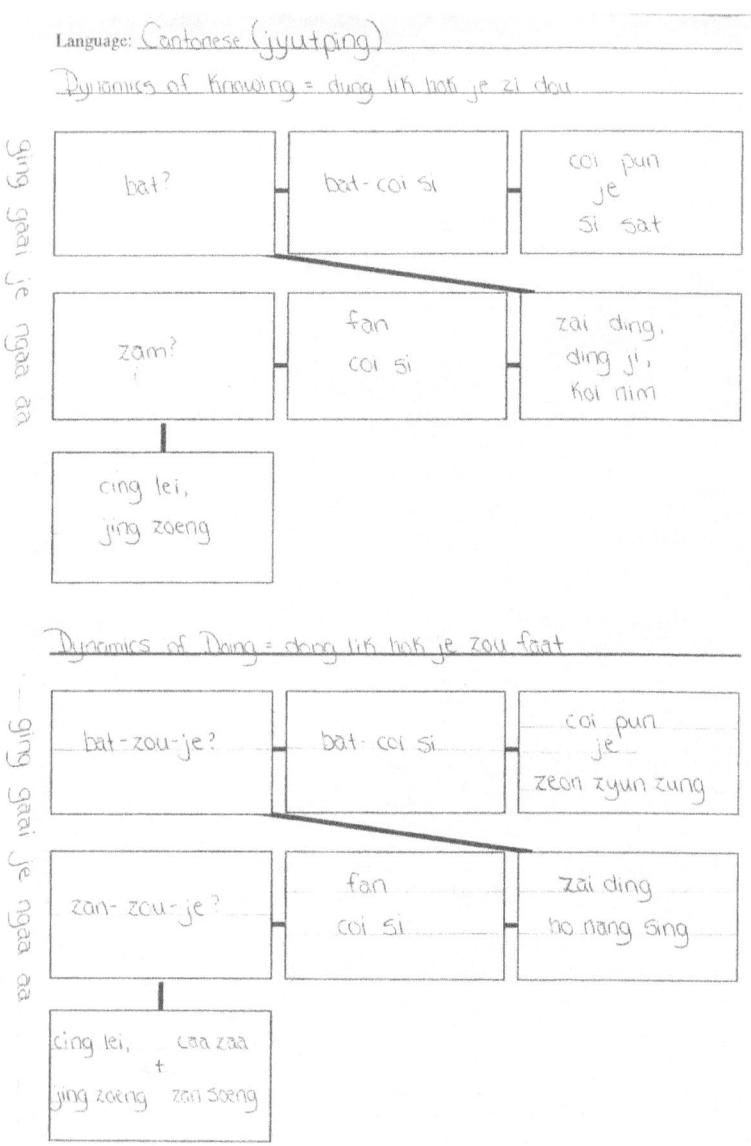

4) Hindi

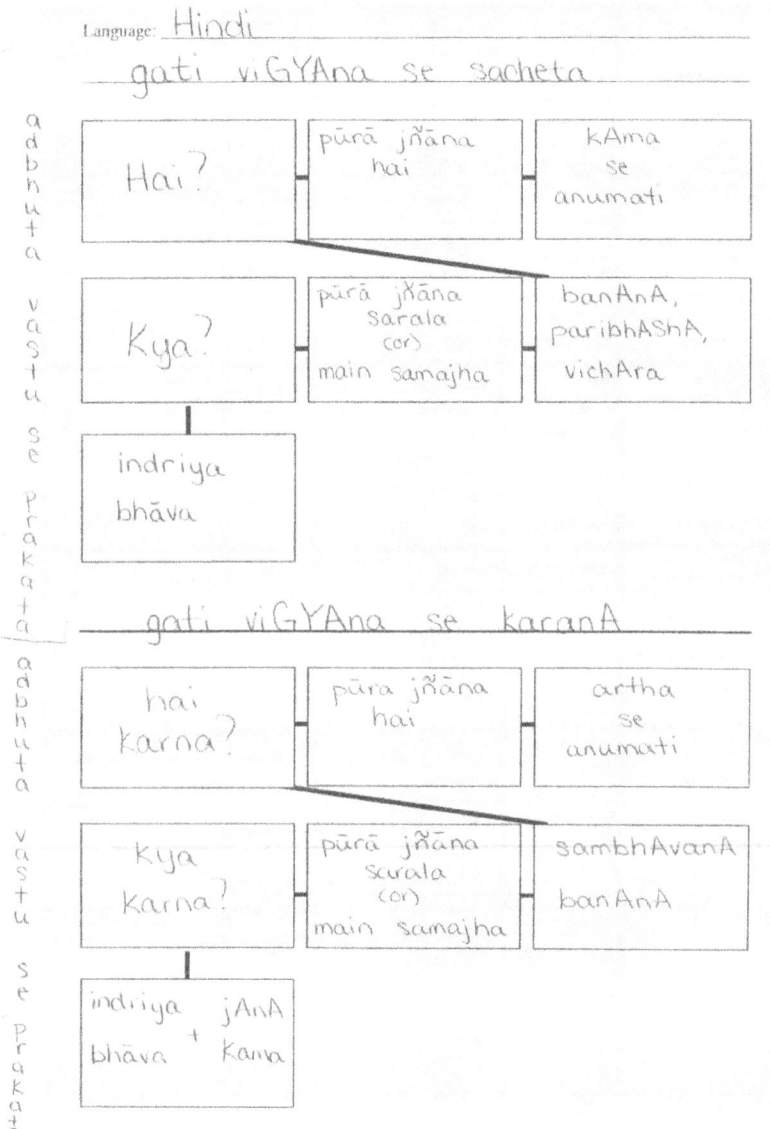

5) Mandarin

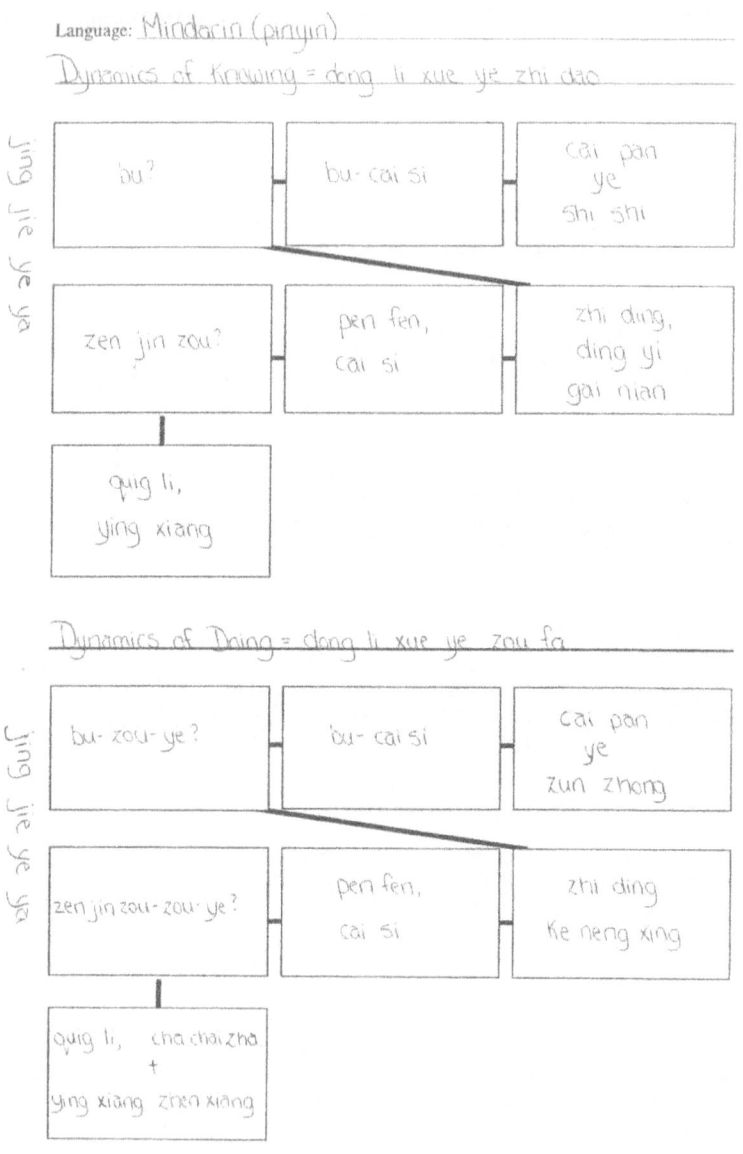

6) Polish

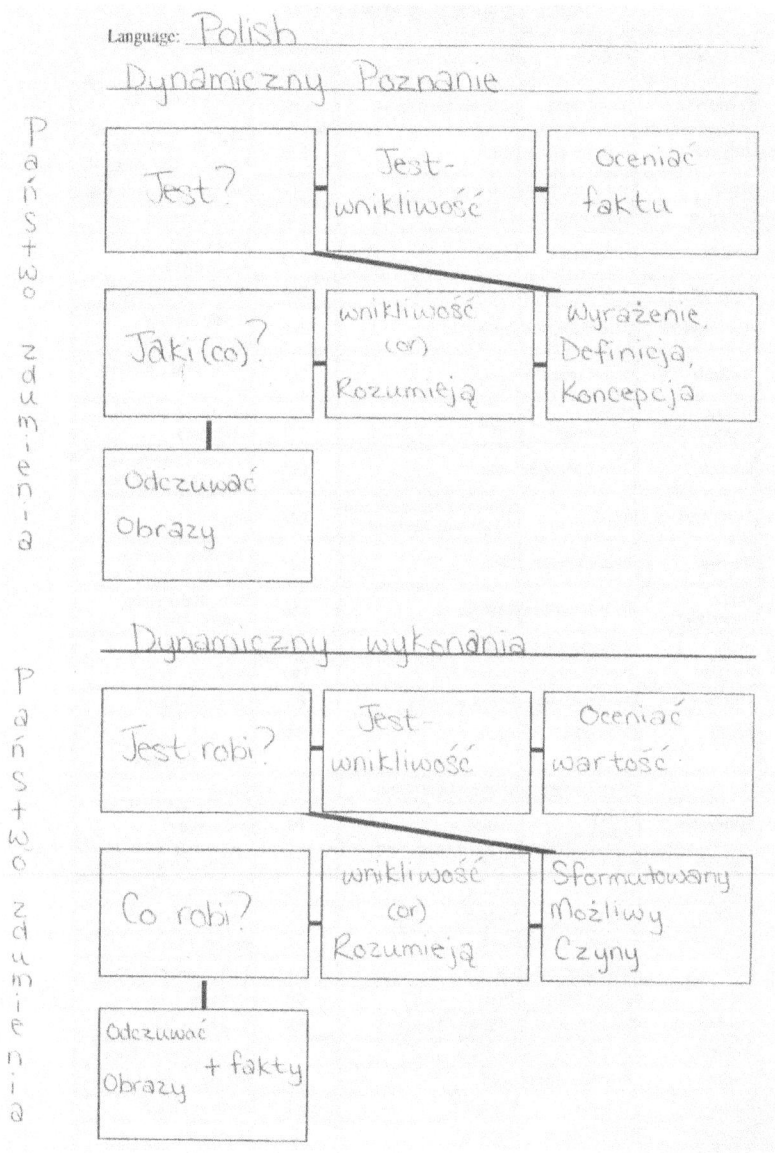

7) Portuguese

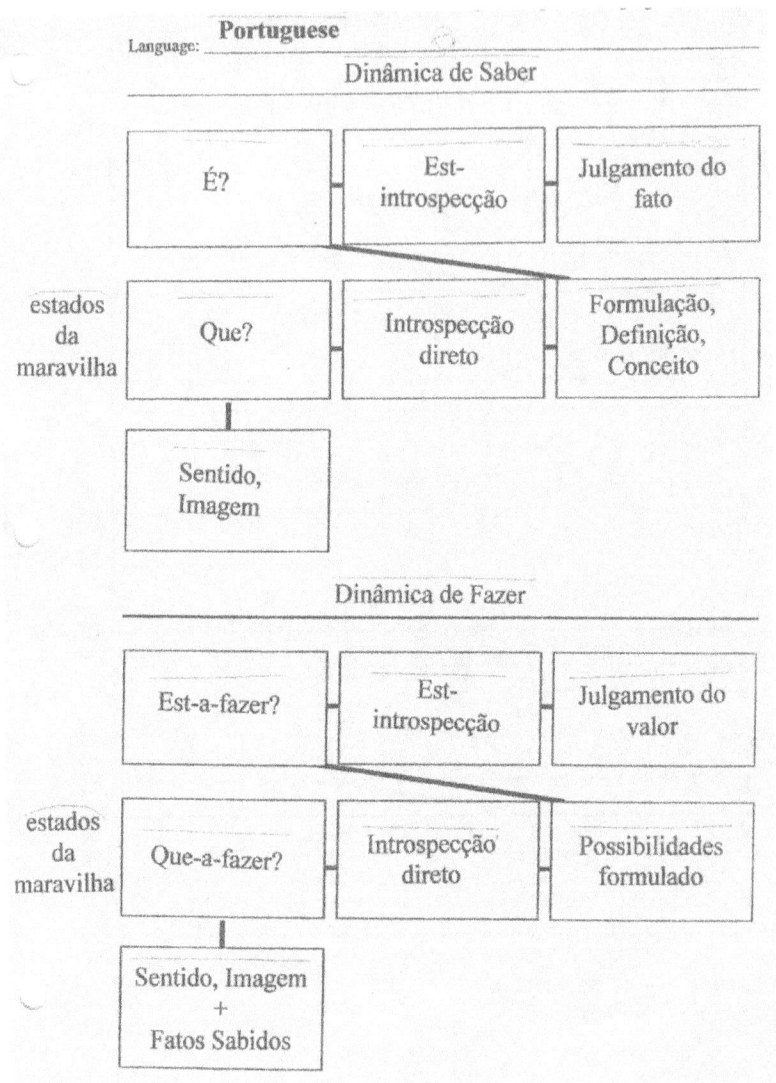

8) Punjabi

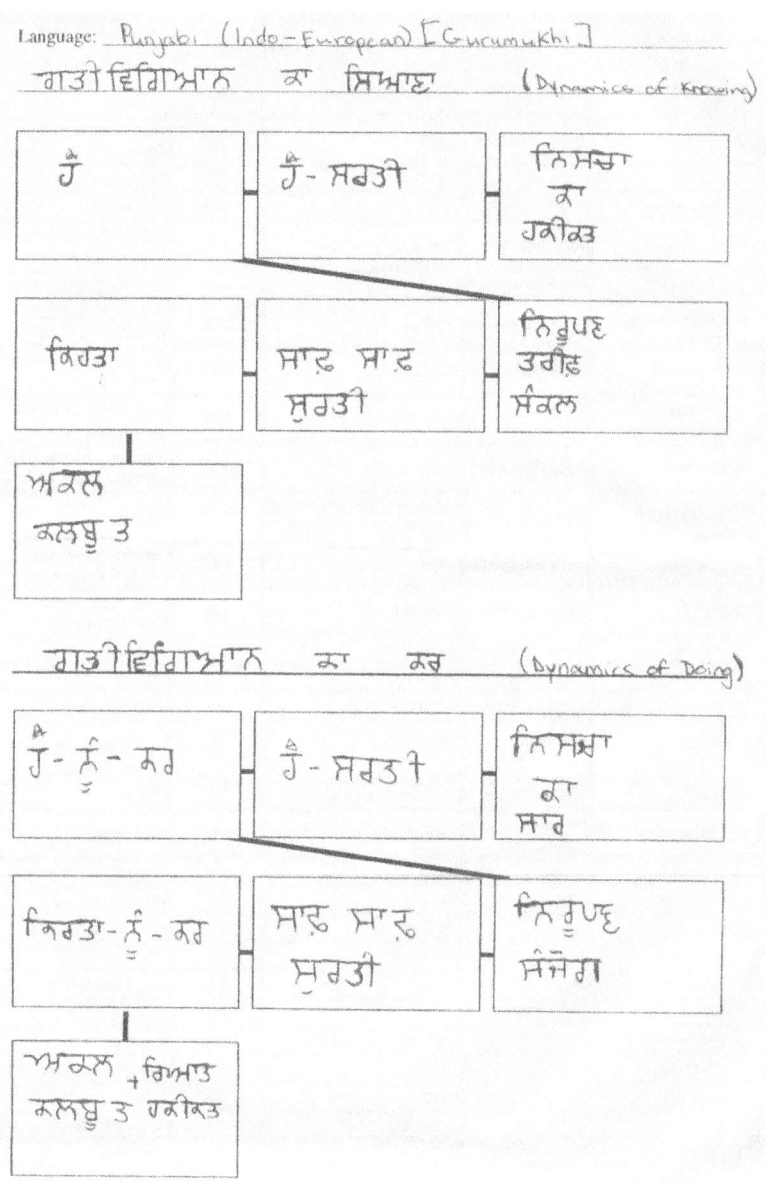

9) Russian

Language: Russian

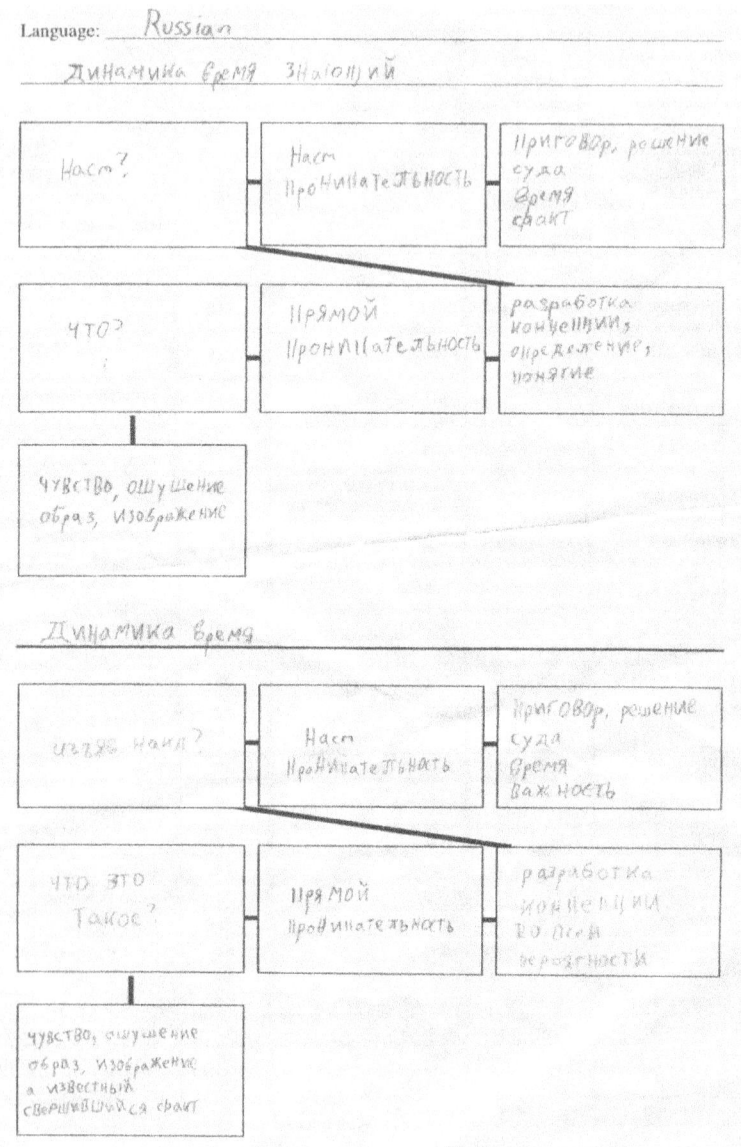

10) Spanish

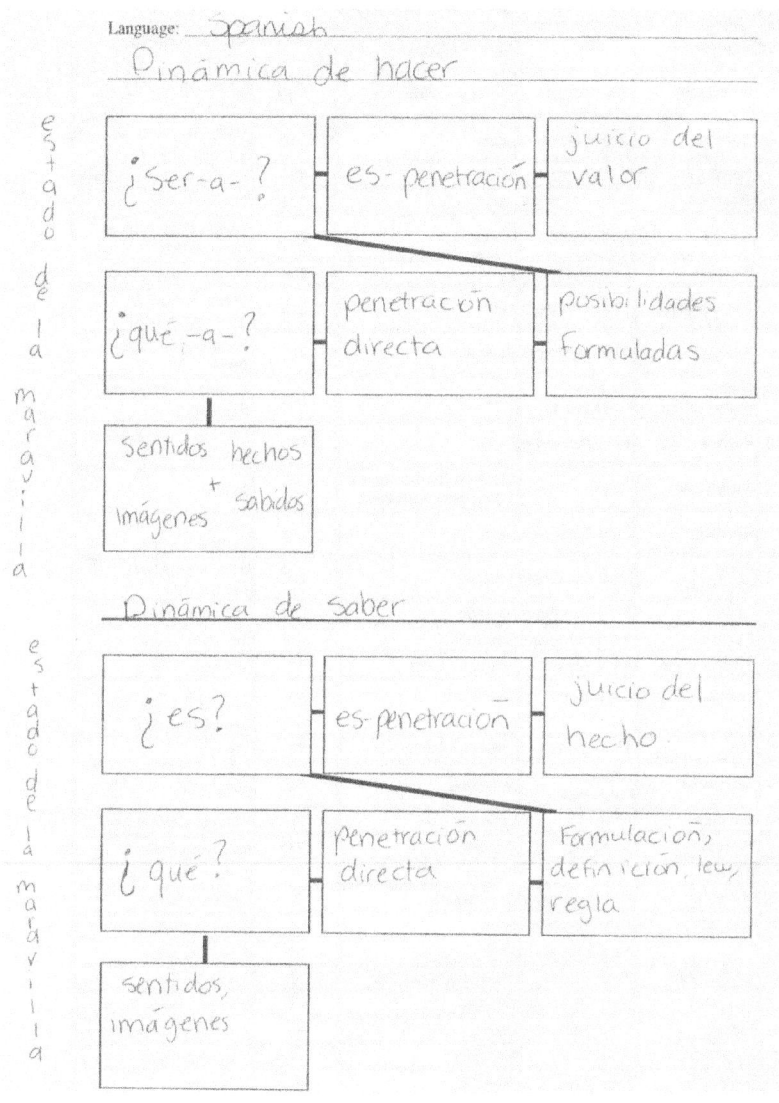

11) Thai

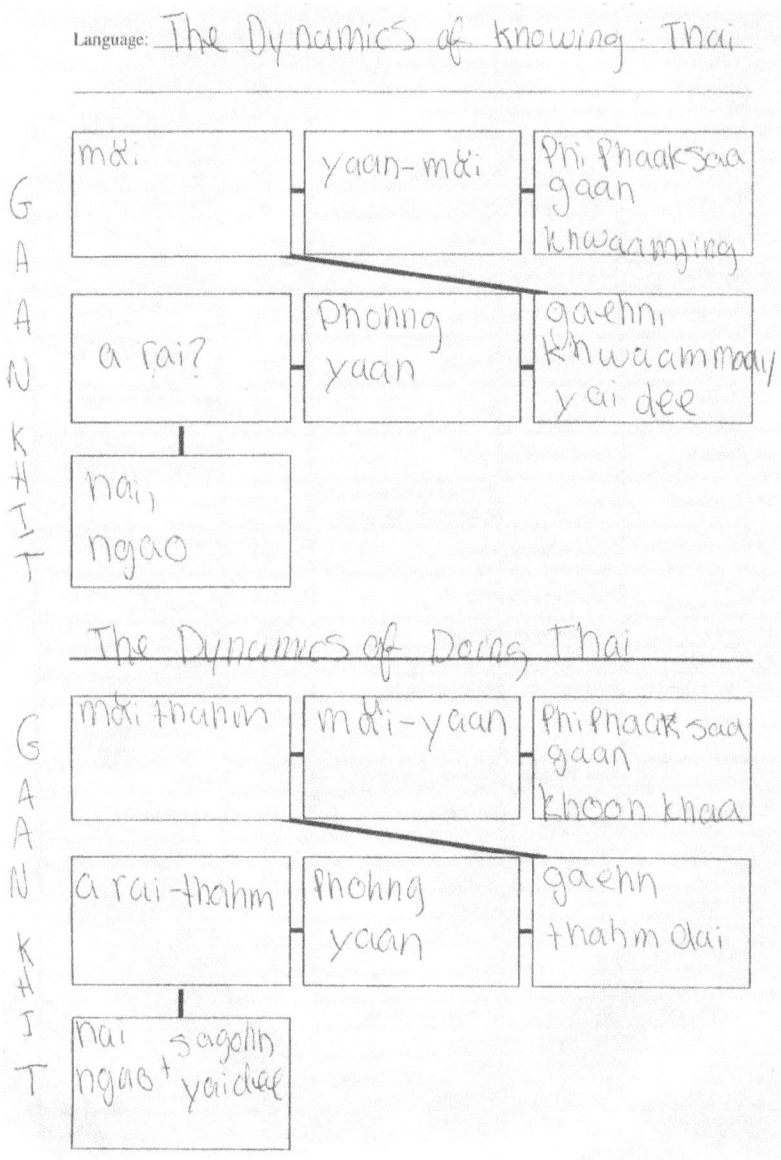

12) Urdu

Language: Urdu Script

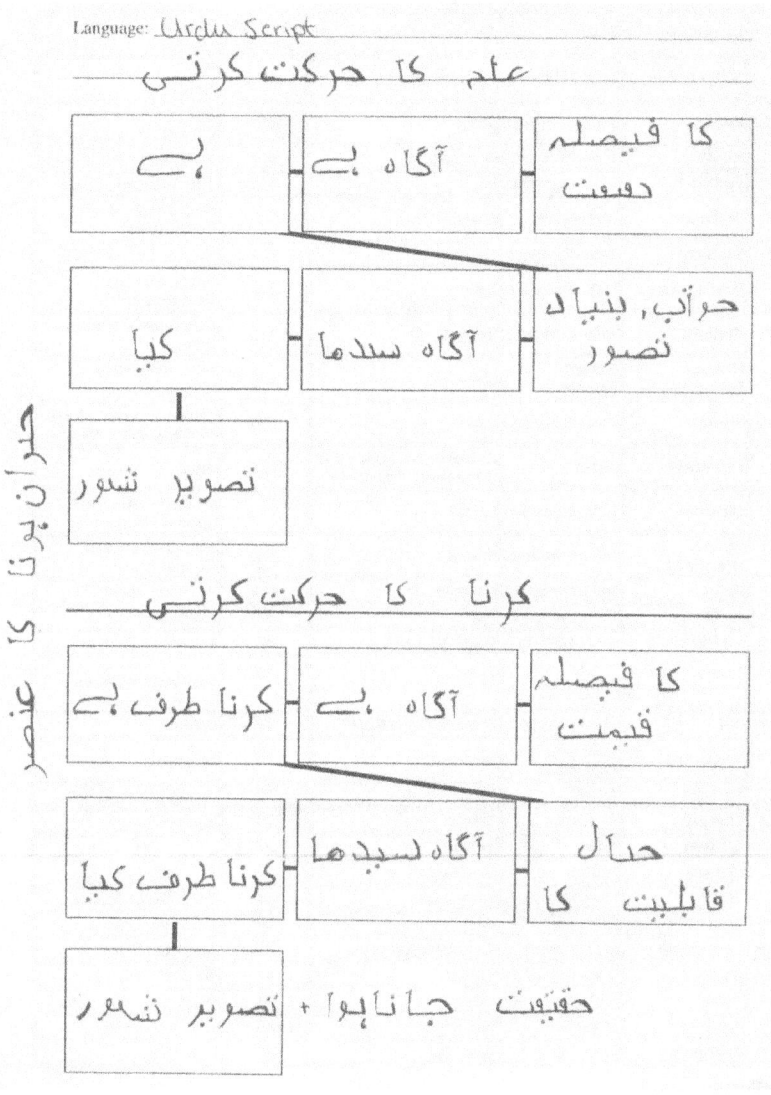

13. Welsh

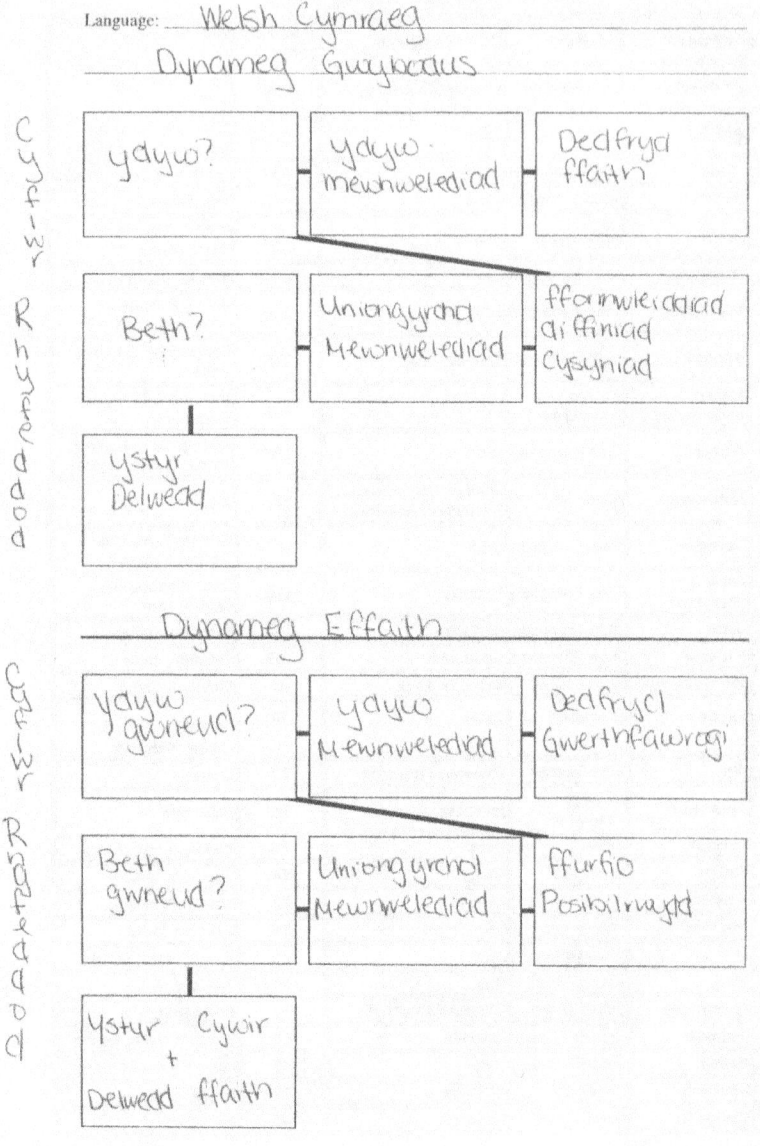

Appendix B

Ahrenberg's Random Classifications:*

The Inquisitive predicates can be divided into three classes as follows:[1]

I. INQUISITIVE PREDICATES.

(a) Predicates of Dialogical Acts.

Swedish: *fråga, fråga ut om, förhöra om, undra, spörja*.
English: *ask, question, inquire*.

(b) Predicates of Mental Acts.

Swedish: *undra, fråga sig, fundera över/på, tänka över/på*.
English: *wonder, ask oneself, ponder, consider*.

(c) Predicates of Investigative Acts.

Swedish: *undersöka, utreda, studera, forska i/om, räkna på, pröva, överväga*.
English: *investigate, study, test, consider*.

Closely related to the Inquisitive predicates in terms of the interpretation they impose on a Wh-complement are the following groups of predicates:

II. DELIBERATIVE PREDICATES.

(a) Overt deliberations.

Swedish: *avgöra, bestämma, besluta, fatta beslut om, fastställa, välja*.
English: *decide, choose*.

---

[1] For each class I give a list of Swedish and English predicates that belong to the class. The Swedish list is fairly comprehensive and the predicates have been checked for their ability to take the type of Wh-complements under discussion. The English predicates on the other hand are given only as illustrations of the meaning of predicates in the class.

---

* Op. cit., Ahrenberg, pp. 205-211.

(b) Mental deliberations.

Swedish: *fundera på/över, tänka på/över, bestämma sig för, välja, ta ställning till/för.*
English: *think about, decide, take a stand on.*

III. ARGUMENTATIVE PREDICATES:

(a) Predicates implying disagreement.

Swedish: *diskutera, förhandla om, tävla om, bråka om, kämpa om, strida om, vara/bli oenig om, vara/bli oense om.*
English: *discuss, fight about, disagree on.*

(b) Predicates implying agreement.

Swedish: *ena sig om, vara/komma överens om, vara ense om.*
English: *agree.*

They have in common with Inquisitive predicates that the complement denotes something which is an issue of some sort. In fact, it can often be pronominalized by the expression *den frågan*, 'the question', just as the Inquisitive predicates:

(18)a. Det avgörs i morgon vilka som får åka.
 Tomorrow it will be decided who can go.

b. Den frågan avgörs i morgon.
 That question is decided tomorrow.

(19)a. De var oense om vilka som skulle få åka.
 They didn't agree about who could go.

b. De var oense i den frågan.
 They disagreed on that question.

With the exception of predicates that indicate disagreement these predicates readily accept affirmative *att*-complements. Thus, whereas Inquisitive predicates only allow an ignorative perspective, deliberative predicates also allow the factive perspective.

(20) Det avgjordes att Erik skulle få åka. *It was decided that E. could go.*
(21) De var eniga om att Erik skulle få åka. *They agreed that E. could go.*

Another point of difference with the Inquisitive predicates is in the nature of the

(27) Nu minns jag inte längre vad han hette.
I don't remember anymore what his name was.

cf. Nu minns jag inte längre att han hette Fredrik.
I don't remember anymore that he was called Fredrik.

The cognitive, factive predicates include the following subclasses.

IV. PREDICATES OF THE AVAILABILITY OF FACTS.

(a) Knowledge predicates.

Swedish: *veta, känna till, ana, ha reda på, vara medveten om, ha klart för sig.*
English: *know, be aware.*

(b) Predicates of understanding.

Swedish: *förstå, fatta, inse, begripa.*
English: *understand, realize.*

(c) Predicates of memory.

Swedish: *komma ihåg, minnas, glömma.*
English: *remember, forget.*

(d) Predicates relating to signs and sources of information.

Swedish: *visa, utvisa, ange, antyda, illustrera, ge exempel på, dölja.*
English: *show, indicate, illustrate, conceal.*

(e) Impersonal predicates.

Swedish: *märkas, synas, höras, kännas, framgå, vara en gåta.*
English: *be known, be unknown, be a mystery, be seen.*

V. PREDICATES RELATING TO THE ACQUISITION AND UNLEARNING OF FACTS.

(a) Personal predicates of cognitive events.

Swedish: *komma på, komma underfund med, få reda på, bli medveten om, få veta, inse, förstå, begripa, fatta, få klart för sig.*
English: *find out, get to know, realize.*

173

(b) Impersonal predicates of cognitive events.

Swedish: *stå klart för, gå upp för, visa sig.*
English: *be clear to, appear (to).*

(c) Predicates of memory events.

Swedish: *komma ihåg, minnas, dra sig till minnes, erinra sig, glömma, tappa bort.*
English: *remember, forget.*

(d) Predicates of perception.

Swedish: *se, höra, känna, känna på sig, märka, uppfatta, lägga märke till, upptäcka, uppmärksamma, bli varse.*
English: *see, hear, feel, notice, discover.*

(e) Predicates of Active Acquisition.

Swedish: *se efter, titta efter, känna efter, höra efter, kontrollera, kolla upp, slå upp, ta reda på, lista ut, räkna ut.*
English: *check, find out, make out.*

(f) Predicates of attentive perception.

Swedish: *observera, iaktta, ge akt på, lära sig.*
English: *observe, notice, learn.*

WORDS	CATEGORY	GLOSS
vem	N	who
vad	N, DET	what
vems	N[Gen]	whose, of whom
vilk-en/-et/-a	DET, N	which
hur	A	how
hurdan/-t/-a	A	what kind of
hur	AA	how
hur	P[Adv]	how
var	P[Adv]	where
vart	P[Adv]	where (to)
varifrån	P[Adv]	where (from)
när	P[Adv]	when
varför	P[Adv]	why

Table 3: *Interrogative Wh-words of Swedish.*

174

Appendix C

Lederer's Random Classifications[*]

The German stem *welch-* is declined like a strong adjective, i.e. with the endings of the definite article: nom. *welcher/welche/welches*; masc. acc. *welchen*; masc. and neuter gen. *welches* and fem. sing. *welcher*; masc. and neuter dative *welchem* and fem. *welcher*; plural (all genders) nom. acc. *welche*, gen. *welcher*, dat. *welchen*. Occasionally the uninflected form *welch* occurs either for the neuter *welches* in the question *welch ist . . . ?* 'which is . . . ?' and in exclamations for 'what a . . .', but *welches Glück!* is the usual form for 'what luck!' (note *wie schade!* for 'what a pity!'). The German forms *welcher* etc. correspond to (1) 'which' in a question asking for a selection to be made within a limited set and (2) 'what' asking for a description or characterization. Occasionally *was für* is equivalent, but with a slightly different nuance, e.g. *welchen Sport treiben Sie?* 'which of the various sports do you go in for?' *was für Sport treiben Sie?* 'what sort of sports . . . ?' The following phrases with *welch-* are of practical utility: *welche Marke?* 'what brand (make)?', *welche [Kragen] nummer?* 'what size [collar]?', *welcher Unterschied besteht zwischen A und B?* 'what difference is there between A and B?', *welche Art von Film?* 'what kind (type) of film?', *welche Wirkung?* 'what effect?', *welchen Zweck hat . . . ?*, 'what is the purpose (point) of . . . ?', *welcher Prozentsatz?* 'what percentage?', *welcher Nationalität ist er?* (gen. case) 'of what nationality is he?'. There are many instances of prepositions with *welche*—e.g. *in welcher Höhe (Tiefe)?* 'at what height (depth)?', *bei (unter) welchem Druck?* 'at what pressure?', *durch welche Mittel?* 'by what means?', *in (unter) welchem Winkel?* 'at what angle?', *auf Grund welcher Paragraphen?* 'on the ground of what sections?', *bis zu welchem Grade?* 'to what degree (extent)?', *in welchem Maß?* 'in what measure?', *durch welchen Zufall?* 'by what chance?', *aus welchen drei Hauptteilen besteht es?* 'of what three main parts does it consist?, *aus welchem Holz ist es gemacht?* 'what wood is it made of?', *von welchem Bahnsteig?* 'from what platform?'.

If the response is to be an adjective or description English has recourse to the question 'what is . . . like?'. German usually has the word for 'how', namely *wie?*, cf. Fr. 'comment?'. Thus *wie ist die Feder?* 'what is the pen like?' (i.e. is it blunt, or smooth, etc. ?). Otherwise *wie?* corresponds to 'how', and is synonymous with the phrase *auf welche Weise?* 'in what way?', e.g. *wie heizt man die Wohnung?* 'how is the flat heated?' (lit. 'how does one heat . . . ?), *wie unterscheidet man . . . ?* 'how does one distinguish

---

[*] Op. cit., Lederer, pp. 50-52.

Interrogatives

...?', *wie spricht er deutsch?* 'how does he speak German?'. As in English 'how', the German *wie* can stand before an adjective or adverb to ask a quantitative question, like 'how much (many)?', 'how big?', etc. The following is a selection of useful German phrases: *wieviel [Geld]?* 'how much [money]?', *wie viele?* 'how many?', *wieviel Leute?* 'how many people?', *wieviel Geschwister haben Sie?* 'how many brothers and sisters have you?', *wieviel Verspätung hat der Zug?* 'how much is the train overdue?', (*Verspätung* 'lateness, delay'); *wie gross?* 'how big?', *wie alt?* 'how old?', *wie hoch?* 'how high?', *wie tief?* 'how deep (low)?', *wie lange?* (for) how long (a time)?', *wie lang?* 'how long?' (of dimension), *wie oft?* 'how often?', also *inwiefern?* 'how far, to what extent?'.

Sometimes *wie?* is rendered in English by 'what?', e.g. *wie, bitte?* (lit. 'how please?') 'what did you say?', *wie ist Ihr Name?* or *wie heißen Sie?* 'what is your name? or 'what are you called?'. The compound word *wieso?* often implies 'what (or how) do you mean?'.

The question WHERE? in the sense of 'at what place?' is given in German by *wo?*, e.g. *wo wohnen Sie?* 'where do you live?', *wo sind Sie geboren?* 'where were you born?'. German, like English, has such synonyms as *an welchem Orte?* 'at what place?', *in welcher Gegend (Stadt)?* 'in what region (city)?', etc. In ordinary speech English uses 'where?' for the goal as well, the fuller form being 'where ... to?', e.g. 'where are you going (to)?'. In such cases German must indicate the direction by using *hin* with *wo* either combining them into *wohin?* or separating them, e.g. *wo gehen Sie hin?* or *wohin gehen Sie?* 'where are you going to?', *wo (kommen Sie) her?* or *woher (kommen Sie)?* 'whence' or 'where ... from'. Different degrees of precision of the where-question are made by saying: *wo genau ...?* 'where exactly ...?' and *wo ungefähr ...?* 'whereabouts (where roughly)?'.

The interrogative of time corresponding to the more specific *zu welcher Zeit?* 'at what time?' or *in welcher Periode?* is *wann?*, 'when', e.g. *wann kommt er?* 'when is he coming?'. To indicate the limit of time conveyed in English by 'till' or 'by' the expression *bis wann?* may be used, e.g. *bis wann bleibt er?* 'till when is he staying?', *bis wann bekomme ich es?* 'by what time can I have it?' (answer: *bis Freitag* 'by Friday'), cf. *seit wann wohnt er hier?* 'since when has he been living here?'.

The word WHY? in English and its equivalent *warum?* in

German is both retrospective to the cause and prospective to the purpose. The more specific phrase for cause is *aus welchem Grunde?* 'for what reason?' and for purpose is *zu welchem Zwecke?* 'for what purpose?'. Examples of *warum* in both functions are: *warum sagen Sie das?* 'why do you say that?' and *warum (wozu) kommt er morgen?* 'why is he coming tomorrow?' 'what is he ... for?'.

www.ingramcontent.com/pod-product-compliance
Lightning Source LLC
LaVergne TN
LVHW051632080426
835511LV00016B/2309